TRIBAL WOMEN WORKERS

A Study of Young Migrants

TRIBAL WOMEN WORKERS

A Study of Young Migrants

Jayanti Alam

Raj Publications
Delhi-110009 (INDIA)

Published by :
Smt. Poonam Goel
for **Raj Publications,**
R-115/2 Model Town-III,
Delhi-110009
Phone-7466486, Fax-011-3212086

First Published in 2000

ISBN-81-86208-13-5

Laser Typesetting by:
Aarati Computers,
F-11/12, Model Town,
Delhi-9
Ph. 7240075

PRINTED IN INDIA

Contents

Preface

It is, primarily, a study of the socio-economic conditions of the tribal women who have migrated to Delhi from Chhotanagpur in search of a livelihood and have found a somewhat satisfactory answer from working in the various urban unorganized sectors. I have also tried to look into the impact of the changed circumstances, living conditions and a completely different alien value-system on these hapless migrants. The purpose is to make our readers conscious of the devastating effects of "development" in a capitalist mode of production, where human beings *also* become a means to development and not its beneficiaries. The motivation behind this kind of work came as a result of my day to day interaction and work with them, and for them.

The hard data to support this framework was ably collected by Sr. Shalini SCN (who was emmotionally and actively involved with the existential problems of the dispossessed tribals from the Ranchi area) and Francisca, one of the tribal women leaders. The method adopted was field-level enquiries on the basis of set questionnaires (incorporated in the Appendix).

In my attempt to understand the socio-economic conditions of the young tribal women from Chhotanagpur and the causes and consequences of their migration, my heartfelt thanks goes to those girls who had migrated to Delhi and were working as domestic workers being part of the Delhi Domestic Women Workers Forum. The experiences and insights thus gained were varied, interesting and useful. I could not have completed this work if not for their eager cooperation and the strenuous work of on-the-spot survey taken up by Sr. Shalini S.C.N. and Ms. Francisca Barla. I have no words to thank them.

I would like to express my gratitude to Babu (former librarian at ISI library). He was very helpful in searching out books and journals for me. I got similar co-operation from the staff of Nehru Memorial Museum and Library.

My special thanks goes to Prof. Ravinder Kumar, former Director of NMML and the Centre for Women's Development Studies library. My sincere thanks to them.

The experiences and insights that I gained at the various seminars and workshops and through discussions I happened to have with various students and research scholars, from within and outside our country, were of no mean significance; and I am grateful to them all.

1

Historical Background from the Gender Angle

Since time immemorial, people have been moving from one place to another with the obvious reason of having better living opportunities. The settlements were along water resources, cultivable land and trees. Adventurism may be a cause, but the main reason understandably, was food and other associated things necessary for living, and better and better living. Thus land, forests, mines, water and other natural resources became the chief economic pursuits of the "adivasis" (the original inhabitants) whom we now call the tribals.

A complete study of migration involves understanding the characteristics not only of the migrants but also of those who remain at the place of origin.

Migration takes place when an individual decides that it is preferable to move rather than continue to stay, and where the difficulties of moving seem to be more than offset by the expected rewards. To explain the mechanism of migration we have to consider the decision-making process.

The concept that helps best to understand this mechanism is named 'push and pull'. Most individuals have permanent residence and this is the normal state of affairs even if each is involved in a number of circular moves around one place. If, however, it is believed, needs can no longer be satisfied at the present place, then a move somewhere else may have to be considered, if psychological strain is to be avoided. Thus a "push" factor appears. Real life examples are loss and lack of employment; racial, religious or political persecution/discrimination; social, cultural or personal alienation from the community; social or natural disaster; industrialization or urbanization; economic insecurity and in the case of some individuals just plain restlessness.

To many people in the world, mobility is equated with opportunity, and the freedom of movement is cherished as a fundamental right. On the other hand, the act of migrating and the pulling up of roots is neither opportune nor a matter of choice to the thousands of persons, such as the people of the Chotanagpur and the Santhal Paraganas region, who have become displaced from their homes by events beyond their control.

The present study will deal with the second reason. It will look into the socio-economic aspect of the family of orientation of the migrant domestic working women and rural set-up (the community) that allows women to migrate independently. The aim here is to outline the push factors involved in the migration of single women. The sex selectivity in migration is explained by analyzing the socio-economic dynamics of rural communities, particularly the gender division in the family, extension of the gender division in social, economic and political spheres, changes in the family structure and other domains and the labour requirements of the different economic classes. The study also deals with the impact of migration on the families of orientation. This incorporates, comparison of their past socio-economic and cultural standards to their present situation.

The samples studied were collected from Chhotanagpur and Santhal Parganas. Three districts were covered (Ranchi, Gumla and Dumka). Bhagalpur was also studied despite the fact that the inhabitants are non-tribals, because a large number of tribals have migrated there in search of job or education. The three tribal groups include the Oraons, the Mundas and the Santhals. The tribals of Chhotanagpur and the Santhal Parganas differ not only from the non-tribal populations, but also from one another. These differences relates to their means of subsistence, social organization and language. Each of these have an autonomous social organization. Therefore, it becomes mandatory to reflect on the tribal behaviour of each group separately and elicit upon the position of women in that particular tribe.

Today, more than ever before, the different cultures and civilizations influence each other and a process of change is taking place among these cultures. The present study will also reflect on (i) how the tribal culture adapts to the process of change and (ii) its impact on women. Considerable attention is paid to the study of cultural values. Traditional patriarchal control and the moderation that has been brought about due to capitalist intervention are of special interest, Cultural values explain the differences in group solidarity and cohesion, which is conditioned by differences in aspiration, motivation and values.

Social and economic motivation leading to internal migration

The objective of this section is to specify some of the social and economic elements of migration behaviour. Some are specifically motivational in character, while others are natural differences, descriptive of the social milieu within which migration occurs. The study is limited to internal migration; it is also limited to social and economic aspects, and does not examine psychological, demographic or other aspects of migration.

Mobagunje (1970) suggested in his study of system theory and rural-urban migration that migration streams result where control sub-system in the area of origin are conducive to 'out migration' and where areas of destination encourage or at least permit, inmigration. In his study social and cultural context of migration have a crucial role in either facilitating or inhibiting the interplay of economic and other motivations. His approach enables consideration of rural-urban migration as no longer a linear, unidirectional "push and pull" cause-effect involvement but as a circular, interdependent, progressively complex and self modifying system in which effect of changes in one part can be traced through the 'whole' of the system. The migration system is influenced by economic, social, political and the technological environments. The exchange between these environments and the migration system is open and continuous.

Having received the stimulus, the potentional migrant will be influenced by the rural control subsystem (family, local community) in his/her decision to either remain in the rural area or to make a move. The urban control sub-system (mostly related to housing and economic opportunities) can help the migrants to adjust to the new environment and eventually to become a true urbanite. Success or failure is constantly transmitting positive or negative feedbacks to the areas of origin to influence subsequent migration. Mobogunje's concept emphasizes rural-urban migration as a continuous process occurring in most countries all the time though at different levels of complexity. In this respect the system approach also serves as a normative model against which one can seek to explain obvious deviations.

MacDonald (1968) talks of chain migration, viz: "that movement in which prospective migrants learn of opportunities, are provided with transportation and have initial accommodation and employment arranged by means of primary social relationship with previous migrants."

Each society undergoes social change which is the "difference between social organization of a given society at two different points in time, comprising changes in any or all the three component systems; viz: the social, cultural, and personality systems (Mangalam, 1968). In the process migration takes place. Here migration is conceived as an adaptive process whose major objective is maintaining the dynamic equilibrium of a social organization with a minimum of change and at the same time providing those members ways to overcome their deprivations. Migration affects and is affected by social organizations of the society of origin and of destination. Also the cultural values, norms and goals of migrants change in the process. The migration systems include all three elements - society of origin, society of destination and migrants themselves.

There is a considerable interplay between the socio-cultural elements and the economic elements to be discussed subsequently. We have to also take into consideration the role of the village community/family, the interply of socio-economic factors in the migration of the women.

Objective

The objective of the study is:

1) to analyze the various attributes of each culture which determines behaviour of the single woman rather than of the man migrating and supporting the family, the factors that impeded migration of single women, the diverse cultural arrangements (rural community) regulating gender relations, focusing on the family which is the most obvious

and universal social unit, within which gender roles are played and women's subordination takes place;

2) to evaluate developmental policies/strategies of the government and its role in aggravating the already existing asymmetries;

3) to assess the status and the power of the migrant domestic worker in the family of orientation/ community - as she is an economic asset;

4) to compare the position of the migrant women with the other women in the villages.

Forests and tribals are inseparable. The ecological background of the tribes has much to do with the socio-cultural economic norms of the tribes. The eco-system has organic relationship with the people of the area. As much as 80 per cent of the tribal's food come from the forest (shifting cultivation, fruits, flowers, animals and other livestock and even the under-growth - the main source of survival in the lean season and during famines); they also get their medicines, fodder, fuelwood, implements and materials for house building. That is why, the tribals try to keep a balance between human needs and ecological imperative and thus preserve forest as a resource for posterity. They had a "constructive dependence" on forests and other natural resources (Walter Fernandes, "Forest and Tribals: Informal Economy, Dependence and Management Traditions" in Continuity and Change in Tribal Society (ed) Mrinal Miri). The manifold resource of forest and its economic importance to the tribals can be discussed in the following categories -

(a) Forest products gathered for consumption.

(b) Forest products used in exchange of necessities.

(c) Forest as a source of employment.

(d) Forest products as a source of earning.

(e) Forest products sold or bartered for items of daily

> necessities can even include surplus edible items (the tribals may even remain underfed for this purpose). The normal things are fire-wood and timber. With the money thus earned, the tribals purchase salt, oil, spices, medicines and clothes, etc. Deforestation and receding of the forest make the availability of Natural, herbal medicines difficult; besides modern education brainwashes the tribals to modern allopathic medicines.

Minor forest products of this region include Kendu leaves, sabai grass, simberi, honey, lac, etc.

Unfortunately, this symbiotic relationship between forests and tribals is breaking down because of the advent of "development", "planning" and "industrialization". The resources that were a life-support system are being systematically transferred to the corporate sector to which these are only raw materials and a source of profit. The consequence for the tribals is scarcity of the means of livelihood and unavoidable impoverishment. The worse still was that a few individuals among the tribals, driven by utter desperation, became collaborators of the middlemen, moneylenders and other exploiters, in the hope that they can appropriate some of the resources to themselves. Thus, it may not be wrong to argue, that as a result of the intervention of the modern planning and development, there has been class formation among the tribals; competition for the scarce resources is now not merely between the tribal community and the corporate/public sector, but between various "classes" of the tribals themselves. This is an extremely devastating development as the tribal life is significantly marked by community feeling/living and equality. In 1961, Dhebar commission reported - "a tribal who regarded himself as the lord of the forest,.... is now turned into a subject and placed under the forest department. The traditional rights of the tribals are no longer recognized as rights".

The "Politics of Segregation", i.e. the segregation of the "adivasi" (original inhabitant) from his/her source of life and livelihood viz: the forest and land, started in the British period. The British rulers always enjoyed the dubious distinction of separating, segregating and discriminating so that their subjects could be easily robbed of their unity, identity and resources. This was the surest way to have a complete hold over the rich forest products and add to their exchequer.

Independence has given us freedom from direct interference by the British rulers, but have we been able to free ourselves from the laws and policies that had made us slaves? Curtailing of the tribals' customary rights over the forests and their commercial exploitation by the contractors and traders continue to this day. "National Forest Policy" of 1952 prohibits the use of forests. But, by whom? By their inhabitants, their preservers. Have we been able to stop the smugglers and commercial exploiters of timber and other forest products? The policy does not take into account the adivasis' need for forest products for their very survival, and the forests' need of its original inhabitants for their conservation. While indiscriminate/illegal felling of trees is fast destroying the forest cover, collection of raw-materials for traditional handicrafts by the adivasis is not allowed! We are also fully aware of the fact that the tribal socio-cultural life is totally integrated with forest ecology; their communication system is through forests only. Yet, in afforestation programmes the tribals are never consulted, nor is their traditional knowledge sought, and trees of commercial value - even if harmful for the soil and the eco-system - only are planted. Shri Debaji Tofa, a Gond from Maharashtra, made a rather thought-provoking observation in a seminar. He said, "Adivasis are as ancient and as original as land and the forests. So, land and forests belong to adivasis only." He suggested that if factories are set up using raw materials from the forests, the primary users, viz: the adivasis, should get maximum benefit out of it; say, for example, if a paper-mill is set up, at least 50% of its employees should be from among the primary users of the forests,i.e. the adivasis. Ironically, the community which should benefit most from the forest are denied most because of the eco-inimical forest policy of our government.The policy-planners subscribe to a pattern of life and thinking that is nurtured by a developmental process programmed and thrust upon India by the multi-nationals and the imperialist powers. We are fully aware of the human tragedy created and perpetrated by the Union Carbide and that is going to be by the Enron.These are glaring examples but the tragedies in Chhotanagpur and such other tribal areas, slowly created over centuries of foreign and national rule,are of no less seriousness or magnitude. Shri Tofa warned that "the mainstream people will get extinct if the adivasis get extinct". This is a rather profound observation born out of a correct sense of history. He, along with so many others in that seminar - both tribals and non-tribals - felt that Bombay and Delhi (i.e. the Maharashtra and the Union governments) do not know, and do not care to know what the adivasis really need and want. One golden motto behind true development is land and water should always be community/village property and not individual property.

Minerals in the adivasi areas, say, in Chhotanagpur, should belong to the adivasis, because it is their land. They should be consulted while chalking out and implementing any development programme. The height of absurdity is that the adivasis are pressurized into the afforestation programmes based on pure theory propounded and propagated by those who are totally distanced from common people and the Nature that sustains them. Commercial and political interests reign supreme; the suggestions and advices of the people who know and care are never taken. The tribals should also be trained and encouraged to be the "middleman" in the marketing of forest and tribal produce. They have to be also informed and educated about the value, demand and price of their products in the national and international markets. "Char" (used in the production of chocolates), for example, is bought at a nominal price from the producers, but it is more expensive than cashew-nuts in the international market. Prof. Ramdayal Munda demanded, "if tribal property has become national property (in the form of reserved and protected forests - where tribals are prohibited and not the contractors), then national property should also become tribal property."

The distinguished participants in that seminar offered very useful suggestions for genuine, overall national development, which will not ignore the interests of the original inhabitants. They are, in short -

A. Cannot separate *natural* resources from anything in tribal life.

B. Knowledge system of the tribals got to be accepted and appropriated for the purpose of the most fruitful and beneficial use of trees and other natural resources. Therefore, tribal brain has to be part of planning and management.

C. Knowledge system of sustainable agriculture is also best with the tribals, since they do not have access to latest technology and the findings of abstract research and are guided by "down-to-earth" realities and experiences. They are the children of Nature and are, therefore, aware of all its moods and requirements.

D. Education system, too, should be geared towards the protection and preservation of forests and natural resources, as well as to the needs of those whose survival depends on these.

E. Natural system got destroyed, because the adivasis got alienated and marginalised. They got doubly marginalised because of privatization and the dominance of the market economy; the tribals feel totally uprooted in the present day reigning culture of cash-economy. So, they feel their culture and identity got to be saved at any cost; otherwise, they will remain ever-exploited.

F. Regional differences got to be recognized, as some tribals are, or get, more marginalised/exploited than others. The policy of that particular State and the attitude of the "mainstream" in that region, apart from the discriminating policy of the Centre, matter a lot in shoping the future of the adivasis and the nation, as a whole.

An Overview of the Chhotanagpur Region

The tribals of Bihar are at a phase of socio-economic transformation. Before independence they solely depended on forest and land resources for their survival. It was therefore imperative for the tribals to conserve forest and land and that was possible by making it a part of their culture. But their access to these resources has become very restricted due to the various government policies geared towards the development of the nation. These policies led to the encroachment into their lives and enslavement of the tribal population and further widened the existing gap between the have and the have-nots. The tribals suffer all the inequalities, and are economically backward, socially marginalised, politically powerless and culturally peripheral.(Fernandes, W. 1992 (ed.) National Development and Tribal Deprivation, Indian Social Institute, New Delhi) Thus to survive, now-a-days, they depend on more than one economic pursuit and various 'change agents' have transformed their life and culture to a complex whole.

Chhotanagpur has a combination of a variety of tribes and occupational artisan castes. They range from the hunter-gatherer forager tribe like the Birhor to the settled agricultural tribes like the Mundas and the Santhals. None of the tribes of this region solely depend on agriculture; they also rely on gathering fruits, flowers and herbs from the forest; a considerable amount of livestock is also raised for subsistence. But with the intervention of the new economic relations of production & its dynamic nature they have come to the point of departure from their conventional economic systems. The tribals are now either landless labourers/day labourers/ marignal farmers or blue collar job holders.

The situation of the tribals is a little different from the other marginalised group (Dalits). The tribals migrate as they are being displaced by non-tribals skilled workers who immigrate to tribal areas for work imparting alternatives models of style of life, multiple interaction pattern and competing values. The exposure of their region to outsiders has two major impacts. 1) Their sources of livelihood viz; land, forest and water, are being coopted into the 'paupers' system in the name of development and they are migrating to urban areas for work. The tribals are constantly on the move, looking for a suitable job. Migration has become a way of life for them. 2) The relationship between the outsiders and the sons of the soil is of domination and subjugation. The tribals are uneducated and unaware of the new economic system (industrialization) and, are therefore, considered unskilled. They had to face disorientation because of this uprooting and the introduction of the cash economy. The latter had its impact on their culture also, resulting in the rise of nuclear family and the loosening of kinship ties and the authority structure. Further, they felt alienated. because they were treated by others as 'polluted, polluting, savage and backward.'

The majority of the tribals have developed class structures as a result of interaction with other communities over along period of time. The national economic patterns has struck deeply at the roots of the tribal pattern. They are working as wage labour in factories, on roads and government projects, adopting cash-oriented occupations; the loss of land due to various industrial bases in these areas are destroying the foundation of these communities and converting them into a national labour class. This population is drawn into the orbit of an exploitative industrial world believing in specialized production. The entire Chhotanagpur population has become a "coolie nation" and the position of the tribal workers is that of the lowest paid workers and producers. This is not only evident outside their area but also inside their own area. The historical process had been to forcibly assimilate the tribe into the feudal and later in the bourgeois society. So, in both feudal/industrial society they occupy the lowest rung-as landless producers and food gatherers and as bonded labourers. The food gatherers have become menial class, agricultural labourers or untouchable dalits. (Irfan Habib, 1985, Caste and Money in Indian History, D.D. Kosambi Memorial Lectures, Bombay)

The absence of a recognized national identity gives them a low status, low even within the working class and the other producing classes. The discrimination against them in the national policy weakens them further; so they cannot fight against the extremes of exploitation.

The state machinery is alien to Jharkhand society. With the British came the landlords, traders, moneylenders, administrators and the policemen. They were all outsiders thus leading to the exploitation of the tribals. One comes across a distinct terminology for the outsiders viz: 'Diku' meaning demons. We have to understand this phenomenon i.e. the implications of this term, in order to understand the culture and the psychology of the tribals in their present hapless state.

Tribal women enjoyed relatively higher status compared to their non-tribal counterparts. There is no female infanticide, bride burning or child marriage among tribals. Boys and girls are treated alike. Both play an equal and active role in the rituals, economy and family affairs. The economic importance of girls is signified by a high bride-price and no dowry. They have a wide range of freedom within the four walls of their community. The Santhals in fact, have devised a formidable institution called "bitlaha" against those who offend their women and the related norms. These facts reflect the tribal ethos which recognizes the contribution of women. Although, the sex ratio is favourable it is declining. The number of tribal women taking up employment is rising sharply which shows the extent of their pauperization and marginalisation.

Inspite of the efforts of the Christian missionaries female literacy is still low among the tribals. Similarly, their health and nutrition level requires attention. In some areas where they were thriving on mining they have been replaced by men. The wages for men and women are not uniform; women have been exposed most ruthlessly to the operation of market and commercial forces; Unscrupulous elements have flocked in tribal areas in the wave of exploitation of mines and establishment of industries. The tribal women are both sexually and economically exploited. This is the prevalent situation of the tribals in Chhotanagpur due to the influence of the "civilized" society, which introduced inequality between man and woman and between man and man.

Over the years the physical environment of tribal women has sharply deteriorated with the destruction of forest and the shrinkage of the resource base. They have to work harder to make their living. Tribal women as head-loaders are a common sight in and out of the forest; they themselves are destroying forest to earn a little cash. In recent years the instances of attacks on women accused of being witches and therefore, excommunicated, have also increased. Their glorified role as 'shamans' (witch doctors) is in jeopardy. Sanskritisation of the tribes has already introduced resistance to widow remarriage, acceptance of polygamy and child marriage in their society. There are also reports about the intrusion of a gender bias in food distribution.)

The table below shows how fast the tribals of Chhotanagpur were migrating out as a result of envasion by Dikus.

Table 1: **Immigration and Emigration in Chhotanagpur and Santal Pargana**

Year	Immigration	Emigration
1891	96,000	3,33,000
1901	1,79,000	2,82,000
1911	2,93,000	7,07,000
1921	3,07,000	9,47,000
1931	3,07,000	N.A.
1941	N.A.	N.A.
1951	4,80,000	N.A.
1961	9,35,600	N.A.

Source: Myron Weiner, Sons of the Soil, Oxford, 1978, p.161.

Table 2: **Land Acquired/Being Acquired by Big Projects in Chhotanagpur Region**

Sl. No.	Name of the Project	Land Acquired (in acres)
1.	Heavy Engineering Corporation	7,711
2.	Adityapur Industrial Area	34,432
3.	Tenughat Dam	97,843
4.	Bollard Steel Ltd.	34,227
5.	Koel Karo Dam (in the process)	45,112
6.	Subarnarekha Dam (in the process)	85,000
	Total	3,04,325

Source : K.B. Saxena 'Tribal Development in Bihar - An Appraisal Bulletin of the Tribal Research Institute, Ranchi, 1983, Vol. XXXV, No. 1 and 2, p. 100

Table 3: **Percentage Rise of Non-Tribal Population in Tribal Districts of Bihar (1961-71)**

District	Population		Percentage
	1961	1971	
Santhal Pargana	16,52,125	20,32,627	23.8
Palamau	9,59,200	12,17,200	26.9
Hazaribagh	21,25,718	26,88,416	26.5
Ranchi	8,21,052	10,94,747	33.3
Dhanbad	10,30,225	13,10,772	27.2
Singhbhum	10,80,104	13,13,482	21.6

Source: Census Data of 1961, 1971

A Few Basic Facts

The tribal population of India (67.6 million) is larger than that of any other country in the world. - it is almost equal to the tribal population of 19 countries of the world with substantial tribal populations. Burma (we do not refer to this country as Myanmar since it is the name given by the military Junta) stands second with only 14 million and Mexico is third with 10.9 million. It is significant to note that the tribal population of India is more than the total population of France and the Great Britain and about four times that of Australia. Can our government or the mainstream possibly ignore such highly developed and politically powerful nations? If all the tribals of India lived in one State, it would have been the fifth most populous state after Uttar Pradesh, Bihar, West Bengal and Maharashtra.

The tribals are the poorest social group. They are getting poorer and poorer as forest and their natural resources are getting more and more depleted. In 1987-88, 52.6 per cent of the tribals were below the poverty line. Surprisingly the lower castes were better off; 44.7 per cent of the Scheduled Castes and 33.4 per cent of the general population were below the poverty line. The tribal women, unlike their non-tribal, particularly lower caste counterparts, do not have to suffer from the double burden of poverty and gender. The society is relatively egalitarian. This feature is more pronounced if the women are educated (even if only literate) and under the influence of the Christian missionaries. The situation here is so different because females are not considered economic liabilities, and the birth of a girl is not looked down upon. They are considered economic assets, instead. Forest-based tribal economy, in most parts of the world, is women- centered and the economic worth of work is reflected in the social position of the worker. Yet women have a subordinate status in community decisions, inheritance rights and religious customs.

There are 30 different tribal groups residing in Chhotanagpur and the Santhal Parganas. The tribes are mostly confined in this area, accounting for 94.72 per cent of the tribal population of the state. Out of a total population of 699.15 lakhs in Bihar, the tribal population is 58.11 lakhs, i.e. 8.31 per cent of the total population. It ranks third in the country in terms of tribal population. (1981 Census) 91.7 per cent of them live in the plateau areas. North Bihar, South Bihar and the Chhotanagpur plateau cover an area of 0.54, 0.40 and 0.80 lakh square kilometers respectively. The population statistics for these areas, respectively, are 31.5 millions (583 density), 20.8m (density 520) and 17.6 m (density 202). In 1991, the figures rose up to 40.1, 24.4 and 21.8 millions respectively (densities were 761, 609 and 273).

Bihar has 26.2% literacy as against 36.70% all India literacy rate. Literacy rates among SC, ST and women are particularly low - 14.4 per cent, 16.9 percent and 13.6 per cent respectively. Twenty per cent children in the age-group of 6 to 11 years and 70 per cent in the age-group of 11 to 14 years are reported to be out of school. The drop- out rate at the primary stage is as high as 70%.

In the tribal belt of Bihar wide variation exists at the level of education and literacy from group to group and region to region. Almost all the primitive tribes, viz; Asur, Birijia, Birhar, Karwa, Mal Paharia, etc. stand at a very low literacy rate - only 5 per cent. As a contrast, the Santhals, Oraons, Mundas and the Hos have increasingly been standing on practically the same footing (literacy-wise) as the non-tribals of that area. This clearly proves that mere education or literacy does not necessarily lead to economic and/or political power or a higher status in the society. Yet, education is definitely important because it can open up the gate to the consciousness of one's rights, and that, in turn, can act as a tool to empowerment. Our observation tells us that Christianity, along with the liberal thoughts and scientific temperament imported from the Christian West, have been a positive factor in the lives of the tribals under our study.

Ranchi district contains 58.08 per cent of the total tribal population of the State of Bihar with a literacy rate of 16 per cent (male 17.63 per cent and female 4.85 per cent) (1971 Census). According to 1991 census, the total population and the percentage(of the tribals in our study) in relation to the total population of the State are 845887, 1048064, 2060732 and 14.56, 18.05, 35.47 respectively; their literacy rates are 18.98, 24.71 and 26.19 respectively.

The tribes in Bihar range from settled agriculturist like Mundas, Oraons and Santhals to the food gathering types like Birhar, iron-melting types like Asur, shifting cultivation types like the Sauria Paharias and the artisan groups like Mahulis and Laharas. These tribal societies, unlike those in the North-East of India, got closely integrated with the prevailing colonial system, its economy and administration. The interaction between the non-tribal peasants and the tribes had led to the development of settled agriculture as the primary mode of subsistence in the pre-colonial period. This process got triggered in the colonial phase as waves of peasants moved into tribal areas. Thus, the tribals not only faced threat to the control of their environment and resources like land, but also actually lost control of them. The innocent tribals continued to get exploited both by the non-tribals and well-to-do tribals. Women, naturally, become worse victims, as they are socially and sexually abused by contractors, traders, employers and even public functionaries.

Characteristics

Tribals, especially their women, are custodians of a culture rooted in integrated eco-values. The wisdom of the tribals is that the earth meets the basic needs of not only humans, but of the entire creation; so they do not take or extract from Nature anything more than what is essential; their art, leisure and entertainment are in partnership with mother earth. They also perceive the divine and the sacred in the trees, hill streams, animals and in all creation. Earth is mother goddess for them. God cannot be bought or sold. Hence they do not sell or buy land. It is amazing to see the way the tribals have discovered, selected and preserved, over generations, the rich bio-diversity. It is an irony that our modern society, which is fast destroying this balance in Nature, considered the indigenous people "uncivilized and uncultured"! Environmental and eco-based culture is a must for the very survival of the world itself. Women realize it fully as the burden of providing food, water and fuel to the family is on them; besides, they are less lured by the glamour of modernization and easy money. Therefore, development, economy and modernization should be eco-feministic, i.e. aimed at promoting women's participation, and not destroying Nature.

Gender differences in power and privileges is assumed to have emerged from the degree of inborn abilities that determine division of labour within the family. One reason for specific job assignment was the biological fact that no man could bear a child which gave women the responsibility of nurturing the child. The division of labour between men and women seems to be the most "natural" aspect of human society based on the natural (biological) division of contribution to procreation. This natural role of child bearing and nursing was used as a good rationale to put constraint on the "economic activities" of women, for instance, restricting her activity to gathering rather than hunting. This became the basis for women to be absorbed primarily in domestic work and in their role as mothers (Michelle Rosaldo:

1974, "Women, Culture and Society: A theoretical overview," In Michelle Rosaldo and Louise Lamphere, (eds.), Stanford).

"However", G.P. Murdock (1968) writes, "there is a strikingly uniform division of labour in the hunting-gathering societies. The women gather, the men hunt". But even in this division of labour, which is not uniform, the skill, effort or the distance covered in gathering is not less than what is needed in hunting. (Coontz and Handerson: 1986) This bias against women was challenged by Mukhopadhyayay and Higgins, (1988) who studied the female reproductive roles with the hunting tribe of the Phillipines called Agta. The men as well as the women (of all ages, pregnant, lactating) of this tribe hunt regularly. Men and women take hunting trips of similar distance and duration and kill the same range of animals. "There is no evidence of any absolute constraints that prevent women—regardless of their reproductive state - from performing any activity performed by men. If none can be observed then "constraints" should be recognized as preferences..." (Ibid) The division of labour between the sexes, even in the early stage of foraging, is but natural, or an extension of the natural. It is the creation of society. It acquired the force of law. Marx states that relationship in production is another term for property. Related to this are both the control and disposition of labour power and also the distribution of the products of labour. It is for this reason that the division of labour in the family is referred to as the first form of property. (Ibid). No theorists, earlier, had conceptualized household division of labour as being part of the division of labour in society. Thus woman's unpaid family work is excluded from the study of economic variables.

The only point where man scared over woman was man's greater muscular strength. The theories on gender stratification based on biological differences only, could not possibly explain all the other factors used in gender differentiation. Till early 19th century women were seen as their husbands' dependents. The sociologists like Marx, Weber and Durkhiem defined social class as a market relationship. Marx and Engels pointed out in 'German Ideology', "the division of labour implies the possibility that enjoyment, labour production and consumption develop in different individuals..." (1845) Thus division of labour is a social order that is established within the family and extends to extra-familial, social sphere, too. Even in a society where each is a master over the other and control labour power. The domination by menfolk in the public sphere extends to the domestic spheres of women. The command at home is the first step towards enslavement of the woman in society.

The first social theories on gender stratification were propounded by scholars who were influenced by Marx and Weber. These theorists consisted mostly of women scholars. The Marxist-feminist thought was divided into two streams: one school of thought propounded that gender is only a subset of class stratification; the other said that sex is the basic class division. Christine Delphy (1984) writes "women are selling neither what they produce for money nor their labour for wages. Their theorizing was incomplete and wrong as the social class categories ignored the real economic cost of production, the activities of wives and mothers were injustly considered as outside the system.

Gender stratification should be understood as a subject of social stratification. It should therefore, include what men and women do each day to secure food clothing and shelter, analyzing how they organize their work around the available tools. However it must also take into consideration the ecological variables, the soil, forest, mineral resources and climate.

Theory of social stratification, formulated by Joan Huber (1987), talks of "the intersection of family, economy and gender". Huber's theory focuses on foraging, hoe, plough, herding and industrial societies. It rests on three propositions. The first deals at micro level and refers to the prestige of those who consume. "It is better to be able to give than to have to receive", Huber notes.

The second proposition deals, at macro level, the question of which gender does the most productive work. The male cannot perform two tasks central to the survival of any group: No man can bear or nurse a child. The task of child rearing is, therefore, assigned to women. But this does not imply that child-rearing is women's duty *only*. The studies done by Friedl (1975) and Blumberg (1984) show that the lower the standard of living, the amount of task performed by women is more, no matter what effect is has on children.

The third proposition holds true also for the general stratification theory. In any society the power and prestige are held by those who control the distribution of valued goods beyond the family. For example, in the hunting and gathering society, hunting was more prestigious than gathering since the hunted animal was distributed to the whole community whereas the women gathered enough food for her family only. The position of women was better in hoe culture which allowed people to settle for several years; that gave women the opportunity to contribute towards food production. (Blumberg, 1984) The data also shows that the incidences of matrilineality and matrilocality are highest in hoe cultures. Women's productive work ensures them a measure of freedom of movement. However, in advanced hoe cultures men monopolized and acquired more power as they distributed valued goods beyond a family.

The plough society preceded the industrial society and the social divisions & exploitations being followed in the industrial society, have been inherited from the plough society. The rich landlords extracted as much as possible from the impoverished peasants. They were worse off than their hunting and gathering ancestors. (Lenski and Lenski, 1982) This had an impact on the patterns of gender stratification. The fields were far from homes and it was difficult for women to do two jobs simultaneously viz: attend to babies and also participate in food production. (Blumberg 1978) However, the impact of settled agriculture was much beyond distribution of the produce. The plough agriculture required particular kind of inheritance pattern which in turn affected marriage and sexual behaviour. The ownership of land becomes the basis of social stratification. Land is the chief source of wealth and land acquisition permits an undisputed use of that piece of land. Since a piece of land can only support a given number of persons it becomes imperative to control the number of legal heirs. The dominant form of marriage is monogamy, divorce is restricted. Women's premarital and marital sexual purity derives from their status as transmitters of male property (Goody, 1976) Suttee (widow-burning) in India, footbinding in China and clitoridectomy in African hoe cultures were in practice because of this.

Industrialization changed the type of work that men and women were doing. Machines were replacing human labour. Men who were serfs, slaves or peasants were now becoming urban wage labour. There were also several changes that were brought about in the lives of women:

1) Women also had entered the labour market-especially the young, unmarried and the poor,

2) The 'mortality decline' reduced the number of birth per women,

3) The introduction of sterilization techniques permitted safe bottle feeding. All this had a positive influence on women's workload. Declines in the mortality and the fertility rates and changes in the lactation customs reduced the time that women

spend as pregnant or nursing. Increases in the educational levels and higher employment rates enable women to contribute towards family income.

Industrialization gave a lot of emphasis to education which is the responsibility of a family, as the cost of schooling falls on the family. The schools speed up cultural change by propagating the middle class consumerist values rather than values of the integrated families. Schooling causes parents to loose control over their children's labour, too (Caldwell, 1980)

Both male and female have clearly defined relationships to the systems of economy, family and gender. But definitely the relationship is not of equality. For instance, a woman's, especially the full time house wive's class is determined by the class of the men related to her or she interacts with. By 'class' we mean one's position in relation to the means of economic production. Even in dual income families it has been conventional to subordinate the class identities of women's jobs to those of husbands'. Randall Collins (1990), on the basis of this approach, suggests a solution in the form of a two dimensional theory of stratification by introducing two dimensions of social hierarchy: class and status. He uses conflict theory of class dimension as against organizational power position (viz. order givers versus order takers) and stress that status is itself not merely given by the cultural order but is produced by material means of cultural production.

At home the relation of husbands with housewives (as well as of parents with children) can be analyzed by using the class criterion of order givers and order takers in the family. The domestic class position of women is heavily overlaid by work in the area of status production rather than economic reproduction in relation to the economic and occupational structure of the entire society. Then we find women to be involved in production and consumption of culture, whereas men are more concentrated in the realm of material production and its power relations. The class position of the women assimilates with the position of their fathers and husbands, this implies that women share their respective male class structure.

Tribal society of the area studied is patriarchal and patrilinial. The man is the head of the household, though substantial amount of freedom is given to the woman within the family. However she has no power in the public sphere. As Joan Huber puts it, this is because women are consumers and not producers and the work allocated to them was based on sex, bearing and caring of children, household work and agricultural work which was tedious and monotonous but not strenuous like ploughing. The migrant women reverse the situation; she is not a receiver but a giver. She contributes to the economic well-being of the family and also takes up a productive work. The duty of child caring and rearing remains. There is a change in the role played by these women within the family. This new role of the migrant women will also determine her position in the community.

The **Directive Principles** contained in Article 46 of our **Constitution** demands that "the State shall promote, with special care, the educational and economic interests of the weaker sections of the people, and in particular, of the Scheduled Castes and Scheduled Tribes, and shall protect them from social injustice and all forms of exploitation". Specific provisions have been made in the Constitution for promoting and safeguarding the interests of the SCs and STs (Annexure I). Articles 15, 16, 19, 46, 244, 275, 330, 332, 334, 335, 339 and 342, allow reservations in educational institutions, services, political bodies and special relaxations in age, qualifications, etc. Prime Minister Nehru, considered to be the architect of modern India, elaborated five fundamental principles for the tribal upliftment, as an integrational approach. The principles were:

1) we should avoid imposing anything on the tribals;
2) tribal rights on land and forest should be respected;
3) we should try to train and build a team of their own people;
4) we should not overwhelm them with multiplicity of schemes; and
5) we should *judge results not by statistics, but by the quality of human character evolved.* Above all, integration of the tribals into the national mainstream was regarded as the only just path.

2

Introduction To The Tribes: Mundas, Oraons, Santhals

Let us now take a look at the origin, life-style and characteristics of a few tribes as examples. This may help us to understand better the position of women in those tribal societies and the factors behind migration.

The Social Organization of the Three Tribes

The three tribes, the Santals, the Mundas and the Oraons, are settled agriculturists practicing both dry and wet cultivation. They also depend on forest for fruits, herbs roots and flowers - important means of subsistence at the time of scarcity. They also supplement their deficit economy by working in mines and industrial centres during agricultural off-season. The Santhals and the Mundas belong to the proto-austroloid racial stock and fall under the mundari group of Austro-Asiatic family of languages. The Oraon on the other hand, belong to the Dravidian languages family.

These three tribes are patrilineal and patrilocal and the family is generally nuclear, though, in some cases, the married children stay together till the death of their parents. They practise monogamy and most of the marriages are settled through negotiations.

These tribes are divided into exogamous totemic clans. All the members of a clan are supposed to be descended from a common ancestor, a mythical figure, who is generally a male. All the tribes are endogamous and clan exogamy is the practice. In villages which are composed of a single clan, village exogamy automatically results from clan exogamy. There is a latent prejudice against marriage within the same villages, even if the village is composed of different clans.

Tribal religion is a potent force in strengthening the social solidarity of the people. These tribes have evolved a system of belief and practice to cope with the super-natural world. These constitute village Gods, clan Gods, lineage Gods, family Gods, their religious beliefs and rituals. The converted tribals have transformed their life style and thought process and look towards caste-Hindus and Christian missionaries for inspiration. (Sachindananda, 1979, "The Changing Munda," Concept Publishing Company, New Delhi)

A comparative analysis of the kinship system of the tribes would show a certain uniformity transcending linguistic differences. All these three tribes share a system of ritual friendship.

These tribes have an elaborate system of social control through village Panchayats which deal with disputes, breaches of peace and social offenses at the village levels. The Panchayat is known as "Parha" amongst the Mundas and the Oraons and "Pargana" amongst the Santhàls.

Thus there are differences, as well as similarities, amongst the three tribes which will be obvious in the section below.

Mundas

Diminishing land size (caused by the 'development projects) has not been able to support the large number of Munda population and so a Munda has to work as agricultural labour, borrow money and mortgage land to the non-tribal landlords and money-lenders or work as labourers in the railway and road construction—may be even in far-off places.(seasonal employment). There is a kind of functional inter-dependence among the Mundas and the Caste Hindu population in addition to the sharing of common habitat. Besides, the opening of roads and railways in the tribal areas have exposed them to outside influences. The non-tribal Hindu and Muslim communities have lived in their areas for several hundred years. There is no Munda land where a few Hindu families do not live. They speak tribal dialects and are, in many cases, inseparable from the tribals. It is through these channels that the Hindu culture permeates into the tribal areas/lives.

Status of Munda Women

The position of women among the Mundas is equal to that of men in almost all spheres of life. There is no segregation of the sexes. The Mundas do not have puritanical attitude towards sex. Young women participate in the dances and the songs along with men. They also have full economic rights in most socio-economic matters.

But this kind of freedom also increases her work-load. She works both in the field and in the household - cleaning, washing, bringing drinking water from the well, tending cattle, cooking and looking after children. She helps menfolk in agricultural activities such as preparing the soil, transplanting, harvesting, threshing and husking the paddy. Along with this, it is the primary responsibility of the women folk to gather firewood though men, at times, help them.

Women have kitchen-garden in which they grow vegetables for family consumption and also for supplementary income. Marketing is also under the charge of women.

Women do not participate in the worship of the deities along with their husbands. They are not allowed to go to "sarna" where the deity and the spirit of the tribe resides. This is because the "sarna" area is considered to be holy and women are considered impure. Therefore, women cannot even worship the household Gods. After child-birth women are not allowed to go to the fields, nor are they allowed to enter the kitchen or any other holy area till they have a ritual bath after the completion of nine days.

Property Rights

The Mundas have a joint-family structure similar to the Hindu system. In the lifetime of the father, the sons do not ask for the division of the property nor do they have separate kitchens. All the members share the property till the death of the father. The father is regarded as having almost absolute control over the family property, and he handles income and expenditure.

A Munda woman has exclusive rights only on her personal belongings like her clothes, ornaments and certain materials of daily use. Usually, the father makes a partition of his property during his lifetime and an unmarried girl gets some land for maintenance till her marriage. However land is in possession of her guardian who is usually a male relative-father, brother or her uncle. She is not allowed to keep the income from the sale of the paddy, rice or any other thing. Women as such do not have any inheritance right on the land. Unmarried girls have right to maintenance and all the expenses of her marriage is the responsibility of her father and brothers.

Women may enjoy the right of inheritance in special

cases, e.g. in case she is sonless. But there are evidences where the propertied women are harassed by the deceased husband's agnates who claim to be the real successors. (Sachidananda op.cit) In any case she cannot sell this property without the consent of the agnates of her dead husband. Similarly a widow is allowed to have life interest in the lands of her deceased husband only if she does not go to live permanently with her parents or does not remarry.

Like any other patrilineal society the Munda society, too, gives more importance to the male child though they do not lament over the birth of a girl-child. The daughters are important as they play a significant role in household work and in fields. Besides, the daughter's marriage is not a matter of tension for a Munda family as there is a practice of brideprice. The brideprice received at marriage is kept with the guardian who bears the expenses of her marriage. Yet sons are important as they support their parents in old age and worship them after their death (practise of ancestral worship).

The Mundas believe that they are the descendants of Singi Bonga, the supreme God. They constitute the most well-studied of the communities and probably the only one with an encyclopedia on them (authored by Rev.John Baptist Hoffman and other Jesuits scholars). They reside not only in Bihar, but also in West Bengal, Orissa, Madhya Pradesh, Assam and Tripura. According to 1981 census, the Munda population in Bihar stands at 8,45,887. Though (like Santhals and Oraons) the religious and social beliefs and practices of the Mundas are quite similar to those of Hindus, the sex ratio is not as discouraging; there are 1004 females per 1000 males. The hold of patriarchy is not oppressive unlike the non-tribal population who, very arrogantly, refer to themselves as the "mainstream". About 8.02 per cent are returned from urban areas. There is a visible change in their attitude to life and livelihood; they become less opposed to the devastating "development" programmes; they, in fact, get keen on making some easy money by joining the "mainstream". They also manage to influence the village youths with their way of thinking. About 27.20 per cent are bilingual (1981 census) and even those who speak only Mundari, use the Devnagri script for writing.

The Mundas of Bihar are divided into totemic clans; Risley, in 1891, had identified 325 sects. They are patri-local and they pay bride-price both in cash and kind. Monogamy is common, though polygamy is allowed. Divorce is permitted and a woman also can ask for it; but the children are allowed to live with the father only. Remarriage is permitted for widows and divorcees.

The concept of equality ends here and they are as discriminating as Hindus in case of property rights for women. The property is equally divided among the sons of a deceased person; an unmarried woman has only the right to maintenance from her brothers. But, nowadays, influenced by the women's fight for right all over the country and the world, sisters and daughters (whether married or unmarried) are asserting their right to parental property. The women, particularly young women, are becoming conscious of the need to earn and own property. Whether joint or nuclear, family is under husband's or father's control. Women, like in traditional Hindu families, have to wake up even before it is morning and start with their household chores. They eat only after the husband and the men-folk eat i.e. only the leftovers. They sleep after everybody sleeps and wake up before anybodyelse wakes up. Men sleep on cots and women on the floor.

Husking of paddy is considered unimportant agricultural work; so it is done only by women. It is considered below man's dignity to do that. The "creative" work of ploughing is done by men *only* and it is believed that calamity will come upon if women touch the plough ! Women, that is why, are not allowed a share in the family's or the community's property and the ancestors or successors are only men, never women.

Cultivation is their traditional as well as primary occupation; next in order of importance are hunting and collection of forest produce. Some of them are service-holders in government and private sectors, while many of them work as labourers in agricultural and non-agricultural sectors.

The Mundas, probably, were the first tribal people to resist the pressure of colonialism and revolted repeatedly over agrarian issues. Who has not heard of the undaunted leadership of Birsa Munda? With the spread of Christianity in Chhotanagpur from 1850 onwards, the agrarian question took a new turn. The leaders used both Hindu and Christian idioms to create a Munda ideology and world view. They are actively involved in the autonomy movements, particularly the Jharkhand Movement.

The Mundas, in general, have a stagnant economic life because they are extremely backward in education and stick to traditional (backward) methods of cultivation. But, the Christian Mundas are motivated and do not withdraw their children from school. Education has provided them with new kinds of employment and opportunities to move over to the developed urban areas. This gives them an opportunity to imbibe the characteristics of an urban population. As pressure on land has increased, and are increasing, due to fast and extensive deforestation, the Mundas are seeking employment in towns and cities, near and far. They are moving as far as to Assam, Andaman Islands and even Delhi. They migrate with the hope that they will be able to earn enough so as to save money to support their families, pay off their debts and even buy a piece of cultivable land. A positive consequence of this contact with the outside world is that the impoverished and dehumanized Mundas are becoming individualistic and, to a certain extent, ambitious.

Oraons

The Oraons are known by different names in different parts of the country. In Bihar and Madhya Pradesh they are called Uraons or Dhangar (labourer or servant). In Orissa they are called Kora (digger) or Kisani (the cultivator). These are the various prescribed functions mediated through the contemptuous terminologies that was given to the tribals by their Hindu counterparts. The Oraons however are generally called the "Kurex" by the name of the place of their origin. (Sharat Chandra Roy: 1985: Oraon Religion and Custom, Gian Publishing House, Delhi).

The Oraon tribe is a conglomeration of clans with no clan claiming any superiority over the other. Clan name is derived from the elements of the environment; for instance, "Lakra" meaning lion, "Xess" meaning paddy and "Toppo" is related to fish. This reflects the closeness of the Oroans with Nature.

Oroan is a patrilineal society and the clan name descends from the father to son who thus, inherits his father's property and continues the clan to the next generation. All property is owned by the head of the household (father) and his sons.

The social organization of the Oraon tribe is not very different from the Munda tribe as they came after the Mundas had settled in their areas. The position of the Oraon women and the discrimination experienced by them is quite similar to what is experienced by the Munda Women.

The section below will analyze discrimination faced by the women of three tribes at various levels:

i) Domestic Chores

Domestic work, like in any other society, is the exclusive domain of the women; men from Munda and Oraon tribes do not participate, especially not in cleaning, cooking and child-care. It is only when women fall ill that they take over. But amongst the Santhal the men do help women in fetching water or in pounding rice. They also take care of the children when the women are engaged in cooking.

Child-birth happens to be the source of ritual impurity of women as also other women who assist her. However, amongst the Santhals and the Mundas, the husbands also become impure. In fact amongst the Mundas the father cuts the umbilical cord. Thus there is a possibility of the father assisting in the child-birth. Amongst a few tribals it was observed that men assisted the pregnant women by taking the responsibility of preparing food for the mother and taking care of other children.

ii) The Production

These tribes, as we know, are involved in three kinds of production work - gathering, shifting hoe agriculture and settled agriculture; animal husbandry is associated with all. Besides, they are also engaged as wage-labourers in road construction and brick-klin.

Gathering involves collection of various kinds of forest produce. In the gathering process there is sharing of the jobs. The usual practice is that men shake the trees and women collect. The older women stay and take care of the infants. (Fernandes and Menon 1980) Collection of firewood is the responsibility of the women, men assist in cutting the timber. However, women carry the firewood on their heads, men take it on the bullock carts or carry it with the help of the shoulder pole. But there is a taboo on the women using the carrying pole or the bullock cart.

The care of livestock is mainly women's work. In agriculture ploughing is done by men but sowing and weeding are done by women. Women and children guard the crops at day time and men guard at night. There is a taboo on women using the plough like in the Brahminical Hindu society. Amongst the Mundas the plough is kept outside the house and the very touch of women can pollute it. There is also taboo on woman thatching the roof or participating in sacrificial ceremonies in the name of the family spirits. It is clear that women make a major contribution in the family economy but the prohibitions imposed on her reflect the assymetries existing in gender relations even among the tribals. Men have an authoritarian power over the women as they depend on men for certain basic work.

Average labour days spent by women and men

Type of work	Women	Men
Shifting cultivation	213.57	96.88
Wage Labour	52.14	106.92
Firewood collection	135.12	61.57
Other forest produce	108.09	90.26
Others	11.33	63.09

Source: Fernandes and Menon, 1987, Tribal Women and Forest Economy, New Delhi

2) Authority within the Family

The authority depends on how the produce of the labour is controlled and distributed. The products can be i) from the field and ii) from the forest. The products that are gathered from the forest and are not consumed are exchanged either for cash or for goods and the earnings usually accrue to the women. She can utilize the money on household needs and give the rest to her husband. A woman is expected to spend the money on her family rather than on herself, like she will not buy a saree and prefer to buy something for household use. It is the responsibility of the woman to see that the family is fed. The other source of income is land which is controlled exclusively by men and therefore, its products and cash returns are also under the exclusive control of men. Amongst the Mundas it is the man who is responsible for storing and also giving grain for consumption. It is commonly found, not just amongst the tribals, that men spend money on drinking, smoking, gambling. In comparison to the Oraons and the Mundas the Santhali women enjoy more rights as they believe that, "whoever produces and sells has the right over the income".

According to 1981 census, the population of the Oraons in Bihar (a substantial number reside in Orissa and Madhya Pradesh also) is 1,048,066. 11.86 per cent of them (more than Mundas) are urban-returned and thus individualistic and exposed to the good and bad effects of the "development" programmes. Like Mundas, the Oraons are also divided into several totemic clans. The customs of marriage, divorce and custody of children are same as with the Mundas. Parental property is inherited by the sons; but the eldest son gets the largest share as he succeeds his father as the head of the family.

Like in case of Mundas, land is the chief economic resource for the Oroans as they are primarily cultivators. Due to massive "developmental" destruction, the economic importance of forests have declined. Therefore, like Mundas, they also work as wage-labourers and industrial workers. Quite a good number of them are engaged in salaried jobs in both government and private set-ups. Another good number migrate to distant cities and towns, to work as labourers and domestic workers, after the harvesting seasons. 66.49 per cent are cultivators, 18.59 per cent are agricultural labourers,

3.84 per cent are in other than household industries and the remaining 11.08 per cent are engaged in various other occupations. According to 1981 census 58.43 Oraons are Hindus and 21.05 per cent are Christians. But this is a well-known Census trick, or rather, the trick of the dominant class, that those outside the fold of mainstream religions are categorized as Hindus,i.e. as part of the dominant religious group 23.28 per cent are literate, which is higher than the general scheduled tribe literacy rate (16.99 per cent) in the state of Bihar. Interestingly, all the Christians are literate as the Christian missionaries had tried to win them over through the spread of education and the liberal values that are usually found ingrained in the content of the education that had been imported from the West.

Oraon men do the heavy work of farming like ploughing, sowing, repairing ridges, threshing and winnowing. Women do the lighter work of planting, weeding and husking rice. The daily life of the Oraon male is mainly devoted to the production of food by agricultural work and that of Oraon female is collection of food from the field and the jungle. There is no special class of traders or merchants amongst the Oraons. The produce of agriculture is, in times of necessity, taken by their women to the nearest market place and sold in return of cash. Over 96% of Oraons depended on agriculture directly or indirectly. there were no towns except Gumla. Oraon economy of this region, therefore, had very little urban influence; it continued to be largely local in nature and was confined to and dependent upon the local conditions.

Now roads are being constructed linking Lahardaga, Ranchi, Sisai, Gumla, etc. Urban traders, therefore, entered the market with modern goods: Money economy has now taken the place of traditional barter economy. Transport and communication system has improved. The clothing and fashion of the tribals and their eating and living habits have changed and this change has left its impact on the market.

Education has created mobility among the village population. They also, sometimes, enjoy the benefit of job-reservation. The white-collared jobs, particularly, have attracted young, educated Oraon men and women. Young girls and boys have migrated, in search of jobs, to far off places like Ranchi, Patna, Rourkela, Calcutta and even to Delhi and Bombay. Some of the educated farmers are adopting chemical fertilizers and modern methods of agriculture, like the Japanese method. Many schools and colleges along with book and stationery shops, have opened in this region. Their beliefs and thinking are getting influenced/modernised by education.

Santhals

Santhals are mostly found in Bengal and Bihar and are the largest homogeneous tribe in India. They are the largest group of schedule tribes from Bihar and Bengal. They are also found, in large numbers, in Assam, Meghalaya and Orissa and even in Nepal and Bangladesh.

Since the Santals has no written records of their own, various conjectural theories have been advanced regarding the origins of these pre-Dravidian aborignials who, according to their traditions, are represented as a race wandering from one country to another. But whatever their original habitat might have been, authentic records show that during the 18th century many Santals began settling down in Chhotanagpur and in the neighbouring districts of Midnapore and Singhbhum. These people, who demonstrated considerable skills in clearing jungles for cultivation, began to migrate to Rajmahal Hills on the North-Eastern sides of the Chhotanagpur Plateau.

The two reasons for the migration were 1) By the end of 18th century many of the Chhotanagpur jungles had been cleared and there was considerable amount of migration in it from the infertile uplands 2) As a result of the introduction of permanent Settlement (1793), a new set of landlords were created. These landlords began hiring Santal labourers to clear the forest of Rajmahal Hills to bring more land under cultivation.

The British Government made considerable efforts to win over these tribals and bring them under control. For some time the situation seemed to be in control but later on the tribals became rebellious. In 1833 the Government demarcated the area surrounding the RajMahal Hills, including portions of Dumka, Godda, Pakur and RajMahal subdivisions as the property of the Government. This area came to be known as the Damin-I-Koh which means "the skirts of the hills". The Santals were now encouraged to settle down in this area. During the next 15 years, they moved to this region in such great numbers that the population of the areas increased by 30 per cent. The Damin-i-koh soon became the centre of Santhal tribal life. The government failed to foresee that the very same tribals will again become rebellious.

The chief reasons behind were the exploitation jointly by the Hindu moneylenders and traders (mahajan) and the corruption of the police and the court-clerks. The moneylenders tricked them out of their land while the police and the court-clerks supported the former, thus making the simple illiterate Santhals slaves in their own land. As a direct sequel of the Santhal Rebellion, the district of Santhal Parganas was formed by the Act xxxvii of December 22, 1855. This Act was further amended by Act x of 1857 which cut down the district to a smaller area.

Village Community

Ownership of land

The Santhals are not bound by their community or culture to follow a fixed occupation. There was a time when they lived a semi-nomadic life, always on move in search of food. They have now settled way of life with settled agriculture, but with community ownership of land. Each Santhal receives a piece of land by village-decision and also individual choice. A Santhal cannot transfer the land to somebody outside the family without the approval of the village committee and the sub-divisional officer. The family pays the 'communal' village rent, the land rent is paid by the Santhal community as a whole. If an individual fails to pay the land rent the land gets automatically transferred to the village community. Besides the arable land the Village community is also incharge of waste land, village roads, grazing grounds, rivers, streams , cremation and burial sites. Land plays a very major role in the life of a Santhal. In fact their social life, philosophy and thinking, their rites and rituals centre around different agricultural activities. Agriculture is their principal occupation and means of subsistence. Hunting, fishing and food gathering, next important though subsidiary, are considered principal source of subsistence.

The Social Position of a Santhal Woman

Looking at the Santhal laws, one finds that there is space only for rights of men and very little for women. The Santhal woman is strong and energetic, yet considered a member of the 'weaker' sex. Throughout her life she is attached to menfolk and is regarded as their property. Till a girl is married she is the property of her father, he protects her and is responsible for her conduct. A girl with a publicly known lover is not sought for marriage. If an unmarried girl commits an offence, her father is fined or made outcaste. When a girl is married she becomes the property of her husband. She bears his children and manages his household. A wife is, therefore, the responsibility of the husband. (W.G Archer Tribal Law And Justice, Concept Publishing Company, New Delhi, 1984)

"If a Santal woman commits an offence against the laws of Santal communal life the matter is brought before the village Panchayat and adjudicated, and sentence is passed. It is, however, always the husband or father or brothers, etc., who will have to pay. The punishment is always a fine, when the misdemeanour is not so heinous. Otherwise the woman is driven away. It is not of very frequent occurrence, but it happens that a man complains to the village Panchayat against his wife. The matter is taken up; the wife is found guilty and sentenced to a fine. But the husband has to pay." (Santal Folk-Tales, I, 222)

In certain other respects a Santal woman is as free as a man. She can go out alone, she may dance in public, she can open and independently manage a shop in a public area, she may drink and smoke in her husband's presence. (Verrier Elwin, The Biaga, London, 1940) In household matters she has equal say with her husband. In matters of arranging marriages of her children her role is often decisive. Even in village meetings women are virtually at par with men. Moreover, she is not debarred from owning land and can also own certain types of movable property.

The earning of an unmarried girl is given to the head of the household and is never kept by the girl herself. But there are six types of property which she, herself, may keep. 1) Share in any crop which she has helped to harvest. This is prevalent amongst families which are well-to-do but in poor families the question does not arise. The grains which are amassed in this way are either sold for cash or exchanged for an animal or loaned out on interest. 2) A second type of property consists of any animal which her maternal uncle may have given her on a solar or lunar eclipse. 3) Customary gifts like she may get some money when she washes the feet of the elderly persons when they visit her house, or at the marriage of the elder sister she may get money for washing the bridegroom's feet. 4) She may get things as a family routine- utensils, ornaments, clothes etc. 5) The property which she may have inherited on the death of her father or mother in case she is the only child.

Married Daughters

After marriage a Santhal girl acquires a double status. She acquire the rights of a wife while retaining the privileges of a daughter. All utensils, articles, ornaments, cash and/or cattle owned by her as an unmarried daughter remain her own and their ownership is unaffected by marriage. Even the share in the cropping that she acquired at her father's house continues to be hers. All the gifts which she receives at the wedding are her property. A married daughter may, in certain circumstances, possess her own land i.e. if father has died leaving no widow, sons or male agnates. She shares his land with her sisters and if there are no sisters she inherits it entirely. There is also a custom that a few bighas of land may be given at the girls wedding or later. The gift may be a kind of insurance for the early years after her marriage. In certain circumstance this gift is also to make the son-in-law into a *Ghar-Jawae* i.e. the son-in-law living in the bride's house.

On her death the movable property is inherited by her sons only. If she is childless her property goes, to her father, finally to her brother and then to her mother. Her husband may be given one or two animals as an act of grace but he cannot claim them as a right. In case of land the sons inherit and in the absence of sons daughters, married or unmarried, get it.

Widows

A Santhal widow has a number of rights irrespective of she being young or old and with or without children. If a widow is young, the chances of remarriage are better. Even if she has children but is still young she is usually remarried and it is only when a widow is old she tends to remain a widow.

If a childless widow remarries she has to severe her relationship with her deceased husbands family and property, both movable and immovable. However, she can take all her personal property which she owned as a (married) daughter and can also retain land which she acquired with her own income or as a right. She may acquire the property of her late husband in the absence of his kinsmen or female relatives. Children by her second husband are allowed to inherit her first husband's land after her death - if the Panchayat allows. The village can, however, withhold this approval and land is then treated as a village stock. If a widow remarries a younger brother of her deceased husband, no bride price is given to her father.

The Bride Price

While a marriage is being negotiated, *gonon pon* or bride price, i.e. a sum of money payable by the boy's father or guardian to the girls parents is fixed. It is referred to as a 'price' though it has no relation to the bride's economic value. The bride-price is shared by the relatives of the bride. A big share of it goes to the mother and the grandmother of the bride. However if the girl is a widow then nothing is given to the girls mother and grandmother.

Once the bride-price has been given the girl becomes her husband's property. But if the contract fails and her husband is not to blame, the bride-price must be returned. This is done by the person who receives the money; and if the person is dead then his/her nearest heir must pay. In a similar way if there are any arrears they are chargeable to the heirs of the boy's father and if the person who is originally entitled to the bride-price dies the claim is sent to his heirs.

The general feeling among the Santhals is that it drains out the household funds of the boy's father or guardian. But no Santhal speaks for its abolition; they fear "if no bride price were paid, there would be no limit to the wives a man would take". They feel that its a part of their culture approved by their ancestors and should remain.

The Santhals are the third largest tribal community of India with a population of 4,260,842, residing in the States of Bihar, West Bengal, Orissa and Tripura. Their traditional homeland, as it is common knowledge, was the Chhotanagpur plateau and the surroundings plains south of the river Damodar; they had started migrating away to Birbhum and the Santhal Parganas (their present homeland) after the famine of 1770. Few tribes in central India are known for being handsome, mobile and militant. Apart from Santhal theme (particularly about their romantic nature and aesthetic bend of mind) in Bengali literature, an indigenous Santhali literature has also developed. At home they speak in their own language, but with others they communicate in Hindi or Bengali; though out of a total population of 2,060,730 in the State of Bihar only 3.07 per cent Santhals live in urban areas. (1981 census)

Like the Mundas and the Oraons, the Santhals are also divided into a few totemic clans and settled agriculture is their main occupation. They also work as labourers, school teachers, doctors, nurses and government employees. 66.56 per cent are cultivators, 23.91 per cent are agricultural labourers and 2.64 per cent are engaged in mining and quarrying.

According to 1981 census, 12.55 per cent of the Santhals are literate (this is lower than the literacy rate of the scheduled tribes of India, in general (16.99 per cent). Though egalitarian compared to the "mainstream" Indian society, the Santhal society, in many respects, is quite similar to the surrounding Hindu society. It will be worth finding out why the literacy rate among the males is 20.83 per cent and among the females only 4.12 percent. Is it because Santhal men are more exposed to urban culture than women?

According to the Santhals, the world is divided into the Hor and the Diku or into the Santhal and the non-Santhal. Spouses are acquired through negotiation, elopement and even capture, though a negotiated marriage is preferred. Like with other adivasis, there is a custom of paying the bride-price and not dowry. But the process of Sanskritization and the urge for integration with the "mainstream " are making the practice of dowry popular among the educated and well-to-do Santhals. Divorce is permitted with the sanction of the village council. Women, like in non-tribal society, do not enjoy the right of inheritance, but men and women are almost equal economic partners in the economic activities of the family. Do women have any right in decision-making, particularly in the economic field?

Marriage is their most important life-cycle ritual and it is incomplete without dancing, singing and drinking.In fact,their life, particularly leisure, entertainment and social interaction, evolves around singing, dancing and drinking. This is what distinguishes the tribals from the non-tribals. None of these tribes can possibly survive the inhuman oppression, humiliation and ecological destruction (which is destruction of their very livelihood), unless they are protected by the mental and emotional cushioning, which this easy and "happy-go-lucky" life-style offers them.

Like the other two tribes in our discussion, the traditional occupation of this community (spread all along the Bengal-Bihar border) was hunting and food-gathering. But now their primary occupations are settled agriculture and wage-labour. Many of them are engaged in government jobs, also. The majority, i.e. 56.22 per cent are agricultural labourers, while only 36.04 per cent are land-owing farmers. Only 1.05 per cent are engaged in their traditional occupation of hunting and food-gathering. The statistics shows, too clearly, the extent of displacement from their natural habitat and the means of livelihood. It also shows how marginalised they are in the 'mainstream' occupation of agricultural farming.

1981 census recorded 81.43 per cent of the Santhals as followers of Hinduism, (kindly refer to my observations, made earlier, about the strategic bungling by the Census-authorities or the Census-policies) 3.13 per cent as Christians and only 0.04 per cent as Muslims, Sikhs, Buddhists and Jains. A sizable number viz: 15.34 per cent, are registered as followers of their traditional religious beliefs and practices. The number of Hindus has now declined from 96.43 percent in 1961; on the other hand, the number of Christians has increased from 0.65 per cent in 1961 to 1.99 in 1971 and finally to 3.13 per cent in 1981. Are these statistics a clear commentary on the highly inegalitarian social norms and practices of the Hindu society as a contrast to the philanthropic attitude and missionary zeal of the Christian Fathers and nuns? However uncomfortable to accept, it is a reality that the dedicated work of the Christian missionaries for the socially and economically down-trodden had helped the colonialists to establish their hold in the backward economies and unstable polities of Asia and Africa. Even after independence we encounter a higher number of educated, motivated and confident Mundas, Oraons and Santhals among the Christians. Tribals, who have returned to their traditional religions, showed a rise in their population from 2.90 per cent in 1961 to 12.80 per cent in 1971 and to a further 15.34 per cent in 1981. Does it indicate an inclination towards relative freedom and equality, which are difficult to find in any kind of organized religion?

The Santhals were the first in tribal India who had waged what could be described as a peasant war. It shook up the colonial administration in 1855-56. It was a revolt against the money-lenders and the middlemen ,the "original inhabitants" demanding full rights over their land. A separate territorial administration, called the "Santhal Parganas", was established as a result of the uprising. Their revolutionary spirit is now kindling the present Jharkhand movement from the 1940s onwards. They are better known as the Jarkhand Mukti Morcha 1973 onwards. Their agrarian struggle received an impetus from the Naxalite ideology and movement in West Bengal and Chhotanagpur.

The two famous Santhal brothers Sidhu and Kanhu were proclaimed to have supernatural powers and a divine sanction to guide the destiny of their people. They declared, "we should pay eight annas only for a buffalo plough and four annas only for a bullock plough; and if the zamindars do not agree, we should slay the "dikus" (aliens) and become the zamindars ourselves." (Culshaw and Archer, 1945). Political movements and agitations by the tribals at the intra-tribal, inter-tribal and anti-Diku levels in this area are all closely related to the economic needs of the communities residing in this region. It is high time to recognize the habitational, economic and cultural problems in true perspective and create congenial conditions for tribal participation at various stages of development.

Changes in market facilities and availability of modern and sophisticated materials have made a deep and lasting impact on the tribals. Tribals now wear shirt & trousers, sari & blouse, rather than their traditional dress; they are also using lantern, oil lamp, mirror, comb, umbrella and other useful items purchased from the non-tribal traders. These transactions, needless to say, lead to various useful interactions among the different tribal groups and among the tribals and the non-tribals. This transition in the way of life is observed mainly in accessible areas; this influence is gradually spreading to the interior villages, though. But the degree of transition is not everywhere the same.

3

A Preview of Tribal Culture and the Question of Gender

Alongwith social structures,cultural norms and value systems are important determinants of women's roles and position in that society. Traditions also are a major influence in shaping attitudes as well as behaviour patterns of human groups. The emerging trends in society cannot be viewed in isolation from them.

(i) Culture, in a very broad sense, may be defined as modes of behaviour and shades of *value-system* that are socially transmitted from one generation to the next from one society or individual to another. This definition is largely to study primitive societies and it certainly does not meet all the needs in the analysis of more complicated contemporary cultures. (This definition will be used in our study to analyze the traditional tribal society)

(ii) Tribal culture has a *pattern* or configuration. Pattern has a considerable variety of meaning but it expresses some underlying consistency and unity, a kind of over-all integration. Pattern also connotes structuring; but it is difficult to express 'structure' concretely except in terms of some special component of culture such as social organization. Ruth Benedict in "Patterns of culture" analyses pattern to be synonymous with basic attitudes, life view, or value system shared by all tribal members and thereby giving uniformity to behaviour. The concept of tribal culture emphasizes *shared behaviour*.

(iii) The concept of tribal culture is essentially *relativistic*. The culture of tribal society is seen in contrast to cultures of other traditions.

Conceptulisation of tribal culture in terms of its *normative, patterned and relativistic* aspects are useful tools of analysis and comparison, but its utility is limited while dealing with cultural change. But the changes within the society due to the influence of modernization has always been held as generating imbalances, disruptions and also causing internal conflicts within the culture. In cases where the native culture has substantially changed but not broken down, the concept of pattern is usually abandoned and acculturation is treated in terms of categories of elements, that is sub-patterns, such as religion, economics, social organization and the like.

The nature of cultural patterns found in primitive society is not applicable to modern societies, as the nations are not patterned in terms of uniformities of individual behavior, they are extremely heterogeneous entities, whose total patterns are interrelated parts of different kinds. It is only subcultural groups -sub societies - whose individual members share a substantial core behavior.

Tribal acculturation cannot be viewed as replacement of individual tribal behaviour by a national trait of individual behaviour. The tribals, in fact, become members of that *subculture* which has a special relation to the national whole. Therefore, the "assimilation" of any ethnic minority means

1) that certain traits have been adopted from the particular subcultural groups with which the minority had has contact and 2) that certain aspects of national culture have affected the minority culture to the extent of integrating as a new subculture, which is a specialized dependent part of the whole. The process of assimilation does not mean change or disintegration of native features but only adoption of certain traits to constitute new subcultures. But, how it gets integrated into the large socio-cultural whole differ in individual cases.

For the purpose of the study of a tribal society there is a need to analyze its integration at three different levels 1) at the level of the family that is below the folk society at the structural level, 2) at the state level which is above the folk society, 3) and finally, at the folk level itself. There are several levels of integration between these three levels.

Folk societies or multi-family socio-cultural systems develop when activities requiring supra-family organizations appear, e.g. the families unite in collective hunting fishing herding or farming. Property rights requiring interfamilial understanding are established. This economic unity is reinforced by group ceremonialism or in recreational activities. The society acquires a structure appropriate to the particular kinds of interfamilial relations that develop in the cultural traditions, and from this emerges the pattern of social control. Multi-family integration is reflected in the extended kin group and usually the nuclear family is integrated directly into larger, multi-kin structure.

State level of integration is marked by the appearance of new patterns that bring several multi-family aggregates or folk societies into functional dependence upon one another within a larger system. Communities may participate in state projects, such as the construction of irrigation work, roads railway tracks; they may produce/manufacture objects for exchange with other community and for state purposes; they may also accept State rules, regulations and standards concerning property, credit, commerce and other matters of mutual concern. All these have *national* aspects that are distinguishable from their varied folk manifestation. Thus the state represents a broad level of socio-cultural organization which is more than the sum total of the families and communities that it consists. Each stage of socio-cultural development entails new forms of cooperation and interaction. And each stage is used as an analytic tool in the study of the changes within the socio-cultural system.

Social changes and acculturation of more complicated socio cultural systems cannot be by the normative or relativistic concept of culture for the simple reason that the culture of modern nations is not built on behavioral norm but have subcultures. Moreover,there are certain aspects that can be analyzed and separated from individual behaviour, e.g. the structure and functioning of the money, banking and credits that represents supra-cultural aspects of culture and has to be understood with reference to industrial developments, marketing, legal factors and many others.

Changes in the tribal culture

At present the tribal culture is almost at the verge of extinction due to oppression at cultural and national levels. What is happening in the tribal areas is that the activities, that are not 'sanctioned' by the bourgeois 'modern' society, are disappearing, e.g. the collective tribal solidarity which was maintained by tribal hunt, the tribal dance. There was a notion of sharing as against the mainstream appropriation and processing. With this came the notion of private property and the *gender-division of productive labour* nation of most disadvantageous for women. There was, no doubt, inequality of sexes within the tribal societies in various sectors like the political decision-making, and the property rights were under the male dominance; but the *diku* (exploiter-outsider) intervention questioned the very tribal culture which was noted for giving space to their women. Tribal women had freedom of movement, liberty to choose her partner, the right to separate/divorce and thus, the community was more relaxed on the notion of sexuality. The diku often tried to abuse the freedom of the tribal woman for easy sex. It has created amongst the tribals a distrust about the 'dikus' and their culture.

There are many other aspects of the cultural life of the people of this region like the structuring of political power, their judicial systems, which is also on the way out, being lost with the advent of the police and the modern legal system and judiciary.

The culture of the tribals have a symbiotic relationship with forests and land which was their major source of livelihood. With the dying culture comes the end of their various sources of livelihood. The Indian State's development strategy has left them as "proletarian vagabonds", who oscillate between work on unproductive land and low-wages, hazardous and insecure work in modern industry (Javeed Alam, 1993, 'Fragmented Culture and Strangulated Existence: Jharkhand's cultural encounter with the modern in "Continuity and Change in Tribal Society (ed.) Mrinal Miri, Indian Institute of Advanced Study, Simla)

The cultural integration of the tribals and the non-tribals was inevitable. The tribals, residing in the mainstream areas, were given the low position of an untouchable or a Shudra. In this process of Sanskritization, they adopted Hindu norms and value system based on the concept of pollution and purity. For example the Tana Bhaghat movement amongst the Oraon tribe was aimed at being at par with the Hindu neighbours who looked down upon them and called them "junglis". To gain honor they embraced Hindu practices; the Tana Bhagats wore the sacred threads, & abstained from eating meat. The Hindu gods and goddess were incorporated within their religion. The exposure to Hinduism had its worse effect on the women who were, till then, enjoying certain amount of freedom. It introduced the notion of child-marriage, divorce, restriction on choosing partner and widow remarriage, purda. The tribal women were regarded as easily available sexual commodity by the outsiders as their society was quite relaxed on the concept of sexuality. So restrictions had to be imposed on women to control this abuse by the dikus.

The advent of Christianity had a positive impact on the tribal societies. They became aware of their rights on their land and the persistent suppression and victimization at the hands of the lease-holders and the landlords. The missionaries took steps to educate the tribals of Chotanagpur. They organized various educational and industrial training institutions, opened various dispensaries for the health and medical care of the tribals. Christianity introduced new ideas, values and several practices amongst the tribals and reoriented their personal and social lives.

Christianity also had a negative effect on the tribals. i) The missionaries disapproved of certain customs like the 'communal' dancing and the youth dormitories that led to the free intermixing of the youths. The missionaries could not understand that dormitory was a place where the young was initiated to 'adulthood'. The youth was also introduced to various customs and practices which had economic significance; like he was taught to thatch the roof. But the most important aspect is that both the community dancing and the youth dormitory were part of a symbol of collective conscience.ii) Education brought western value system which built a gap between the tribals who hold on to their traditions and those who opt for adopting themselves to anything modern. The education system did not support the tribal practices and declared it as unscientific. iii) It also created a gap between the Christian and the non Christian tribals, as missionaries put restriction on the free mixing of the two groups. There even emerged a difference in certain practices amongst the same tribe e.g. a Christian tribal will shake hand and greet by saying "Jai Jesu" whereas a non -Christian will say "Jowhar". Thus a clear-cut division is created within a tribal society.

The subordination of the women in the three tribes (under study) is quite well established in the discussion above. And that there were many changes in the position of women in these tribes, ranging from the foraging hordes to agriculturist village communities, is quite apparent from the discussion. From the social structure of the three tribes it is observed that there are community property (grazing lands, forests, wells and rivers), and also the individual property of the male head of the household.

In the foraging state the access to the productive resources was that of the whole community. Within the family there was no notion of the income of 'the head of the household ie, of the male.' In fact, it was the women who did the major marketing and therefore, usually, controlled the use of income. There was the no concept of accumulation. Patrilocality is the norm while matrilocality is also accepted and has no disadvantage. There is no notion of male control of female sexuality nor is there the notion of perpetuation of the lineage.

With the primary dependence on land, as the major productive resource, definite rules of access, based on kinship and lineage got evolved. This is quite apparent in the settled agricultural, communities. Access to land is combined with allotment to individual families, essentially to the male head of the household. The lands that are accumulated over a period of time is inherited by menfolk. Patrilocality ensures that in this form of partly communal property, women are non-owner workers. The tribes now also have notions of "purity of women" and "perpetuation" of the lineage, (in order to be able to pass on the results of accumulation viz. land.) It is with the establishment of individual property, that the tribal women looses relative autonomy in her own spheres of activity leading to strict division of labour.

Therefore, there are two crucial areas of inequality - property rights and political participation. Property, particularly land,passes through the male line. All the three tribes are patrilineial and patrilocal. Women are the unpaid labour. The other important inequality is that of political participation. The traditional village assembly (Panchayat) is an all-male institution.

The aforementioned description of the culture of the tribes and *their inequality experienced* will help us to analyze the position of the tribal women who migrate to urban areas for domestic work. The following chapter will look at the changes in the outlook of the family of orientation with the women migrating who become an important means of economic support.

A distinction is generally made between *Sex*- the condition of being male or female on the basis of biological characteristics, and *Gender*- the socially constructed ways of being masculine or feminine. We must stay away from the tendency of the male-dominated society to impose *differentiation* (viz: women are inferior to men). It argues that this difference is biological and therefore, "natural, inevitable and justified." Two persistent facts can be observed across time and space, viz. (1) gender-based social division of labour i.e. women to household activities, the value of which cannot be assessed in money terms nor can it be calculated in GNP, and men in productive activities generating money-income and (ii) women experiencing less access to resources, benefits (of developmental work) and power. Gender is a valuable concept as it facilitates the correct identification of social structures, practices and ideologies that perpetuate and reinforce the unequal position of women in a man's world.

Patriarchy is not simply control over women's body in the sphere of reproduction, it is control over her total labour. Women's labour is exchanged for consumption, which is determined by the male head of the household. *Alienation*, thus, is a relation where the product of labour is appropriated by someone other than the labourer, viz. by the owner of the property. If belonging to an exploited class, women are subject to *double* alienation— first, by the owner of land/property/ system and secondly, by the head of the household (father, father-in-law, husband or mother-in-law). Just as patriarchy has been seen as the inevitable result of human civilisation, capitalism is perceived as an inevitable stage of human history. Any opposition to capitalist inroads is, then, taken as opposition to development. Movements, opposed to this process of development (like the Jharkhand movement) are, therefore, labelled as "reactionary." Strengthening of the village community by providing individual access - of both men and women - to land and other productive resources can provide for a "development" that is not anti-people and anti-woman.

There may not be as strong a preference for a son as among the non-tribals (whether Hindu, Muslim or Sikh), but a boy definitely enjoys preferential treatment in his family. His sister may be eating as much and as good, but he will, definitely, get more time to play and more opportunities for education. This mentality is much less pronounced among the Christians, or rather, among those who are reaping the benefits from the Christian missionaries - noted in chapter IV). The sex-ratio, though still favourable to women, is nevertheless declining. Bride price is slowly being replaced by dowry! A widower or a divorced man can marry easily - not a widow or a divorced woman.

If a tribal *man* has sexual relations with, or marries a non-tribal, he can be re-admitted in the tribal society if he breaks off from the non-tribal and pays a fine to his community. But a tribal woman committing this "crime" is doomed for ever; she cannot be accepted back at any cost.

Jokes reflect prevalent attitudes. "Why do women use both hands to wash their face, and men only one?" The answer is, "because women have *two* lords, viz. Singibonga (Munda God) and her husband."

Correct identification will enable us to develop correct strategies to redress these inequalities. The human development paradigm, which puts people at the centre of its concern, must be fully engendered. Any such attempt would embrace at least the following three principles:

* Equality of rights between women and men must be enshrined as a fundamental principle. Legal, economic, political or cultural barriers that prevent the exercise of equal rights should be identified and removed through comprehensive policy reforms and strong affirmative action.
* Women must be regarded as agents and beneficiaries of change. Investing in women's capabilities and empowering them to exercise their choices is not only valuable in itself but is also the surest way to contribute to economic growth and overall development.
* The engendered development model, though aiming to widen choices for both women and men, should not predetermine how different cultures and different societies exercise these choices. What is important is that equal opportunities to make a choice exist for both women and men.

In no society do women enjoy the same opportunities as men.

The 'gender-related development index' (GDI) reflects gender disparities in basic human capabilities and ranks 130 countries on a global scale. The four top countries are in the Nordic belt - Sweden, Finland, Norway and Denmark, in that order. This is hardly surprising. These countries, much concerned with ending the relative deprivation of women, have adopted gender equality and women's empowerment as conscious national policies. In these countries, adult literacy rates are similar for women and men, and combined enrolment is higher for females. Life expectancy is, on average, about seven years higher for women (compared with an estimated global biological age of five years higher). And women's earned income is around three-fourths of men's income. (NOTE: Inspite of being gender- equal in almost all spheres,these countries are yet to succeed in the sphere of economic equality—women's incomes are still lower than those of men.)

Several developing countries and areas also do quite well in the GDI rankings:

Barbados (rank 11), Hong King (17), the Bahamas (26), Singapore (28), Uruguay (32) and Thailand (33). These countries have succeeded in building the basic human capabilities of both women and men, without substantial gender disparity.

But, it is clear from the GDI estimates that in no society do women enjoy the same opportunities as men. The top rank is enjoyed by Sweden, with a GDI value of 0.92 - compared with a maximum possible value of 1.00 (maximum achievement with perfect equality). After the top 32 countries, the GDI value drops below 0.80 - indicating what a long distance women still have to travel towards gender equality even in countries that seem to be doing better on this score.

Really disturbing is the fact that as many as 45 countries in the sample analysis are below a GDI value of 0.5, showing that women suffer the double deprivation of gender disparity and low achievement.

The countries showing GDI ranks markedly higher than their HDI ranks are fairly diverse. They include Denmark, Sweden, Norway and Finland, the Czech Republic, Slovakia, Hungary, Poland, Barbados, Thailand, Sri Lanka, Malaysia, Jamaica and Cuba.

The real difference lies in women's share of 'earned income' compared with men's share - a clear reflection of the much lower participation of women in the labour force and their lower average wage-structure.

Removing gender-inequality has nothing to do with national income. Income is not the decisive factor. Several of the world's poor nations have been able to raise female literacy rates. With limited resources but a strong political commitment, China, Sri Lanka and Zimbabwe raised adult women's literacy to 70% or more. By contrast, several richer countries lag behind.

China is ten times above Saudi Arabia in GDI ranks, even though its real per capita income is a fifth of the latter. Thailand outranks Spain in the GDI, even though Thailand's real per capita income is less than half of Spain's. Poland's GDI rank is 50 places higher than Syria's, even though the two countries have about the same real income.

A relevant agenda for future action, therefore, needs to encompass a number of interlinked strategies to address the above strategic and practical needs of women in the world of work as was done in the recent ILO major multidisciplinary initiative called the Interdepartmental Project on Equality for Women in Employment (ILO, 1991). Such an agenda should include the following:

a) *a supportive legislative framework and enforcement mechanisms* not only labour law but also family-property inheritance and contract laws should stress equality; such legislation should keep pace with the developments in the social and economic roles played by women and the changes in society. Gender equality should be integrated in the conception of new laws and in legal reforms.

b) *gender-sensitive macro and micro economic policymaking* issues regarding job segregation and gender pay differentials should be mainstreamed into such policies. The effects of such policies on women should be regularly monitored.

c) *education and training* i.e. the formulation of appropriate gender- balanced training policies; emphasis on intensive & extensive skills-training for women, including non-traditional ones, to enable them to benefit from employment opportunities emerging from the technological transformations and to reduce the gender-based job- segregation.

d) *access to productive resources* such as credit, land, technology, markets and relevant information.

e) *social security and protection* extending social security to cover all categories of women workers, particularly the vulnerable groups outside the formal sector; providing good quality and affordable child care facilities so that they can reconcile work with family responsibilities.

f) *promoting quality employment,* emphasizing equal pay for work of equal value, better working conditions for occupational safety and health, and elimination of discriminatory practices and sexual harassment.

g) *women's empowerment through mobilization in groups and representation and participation in decision-making with* special emphasis on group formation among grassroots level women; participation in trade unions, employers' organizations and other relevant organizations and governmental and political structures;

h) *targeting the more vulnerable and disadvantaged women* such as the poor, unemployed, migrant, displaced and disabled, rural and informal sector workers to protect, improve their working conditions, reduce poverty and promote their economic and social well-being.

Human development is a process of enlarging the scope of choices for *all people*, not for just one section of the society. The continuing exclusion of women from many economic and political opportunities is a continuing indictment of modern progress. Moving towards gender equality is a socio-political process. It requires a new way of thinking. The stereotypical notion about men and women must give way to a new philosophy that regards all citizens , irrespective of caste, class, religion or *Sex*, as essential agents of change and progress.

> "Maid stabbed, gagged, bound and left for dead" (Indonesia).
>
> "Execution in U.A.E. of a 20 year old Sri Lankan house-maid".
>
> "Construction-workers in West Asia face poor work conditions."

These are a few of the hundreds of cases reported (or, not reported) in the newspapers. The plight of the migrant labour, whether international or intra-national, is the same. They are deprived of their hearth and home & of their sources of livelihood, which should have been their birthright—the way it is to the privileged and the powerful. The ILO confirms that 100 million people are on the move across international boundaries - i.e. one out of every 50 citizen of the world. We do not know for sure how many millions are fated to migrate *within their own countries*. The consequences are alarming:-

a) They are, invariably paid less and are expected to do the least desirable and most difficult, dangerous and dirty jobs.

b) They experience discriminations and cultural dislocation.

c) What is less known and not properly documented is that migrant workers are habitually the victims of the worst forms of abuse (like theft, rape and even death) by the employers with the complicity of the police and the government officials, and the victims seldom get justice from the judiciary, even. (But lately,to our great satisfaction and happiness,the judiciary ,particularly the Supreme Court,is acting gender-sensitive and gender-just. The gates are slowly opening up for the 'inferior' sex.)

d) Women migrant workers, invariably turn out to be the worst victims. In case of international migration, the home - governments encourage them to work outside so that the government can earn precious foreign currency. But the governments fail to negotiate with or pressurize the employing governments in case of abuse of the workers' human dignity. For example, Government of India lured young girls from the North-East, West Bengal and Goa to migrate to Singapore as domestic workers while those from Philippines quit in protest against similar governmental policy and activity.

The United Nations statistics show women are

* 70% of the world's poorest (billion) people

* working for two-third of humanity's labouring hours
* getting only one-tenths of the world's income
* owning only one per cent of the world's property
* the majority of the world's illiterates
* 75% of the world's 18 million refugees.

In India female labour force participation rates are higher among women belonging to the scheduled castes and the scheduled tribes. They account for nearly half of all female agricultural labourers while they constitute only about a quarter of India's rural female population. Another feature of the seventies was the increase in the female child labour. (Swaminathan, 1994).

4

Socio-Economic Causes of Migration

Before we go into the causes behind migrations and the socio-economic conditions of the migrants and migrant-families, we must look, briefly, into the overall economic conditions of the tribals under our study.

South Bihar is the habitat of more than six million tribals and is rich in forest and mineral resources. Yet, the average per day per capita income of a tribal family in Palamau, Santhal Pargana, Singhbhum, Ranchi, Hazaribagh, etc. did not exceed the inhumanly low amount of Rs.1.50. Facilities for pure drinking water and roads are a far cry even today. A few among them, yet, are emerging as the middle class, due to a reasonably high level of education and contact with the modern world. (NG Basu, "Tribals and Democracy in India", Mainstream, 19.12.87) We shall discuss later why and how Christianity had offered the converts easier access to education and why and how education paved the way for better job opportunities, particularly in the urban areas.

Chowdhary and Bhattacharjee, in a study conducted for Agro-Economic Research Centre, Vishwa Bharati (1976), found that per capita weekly consumption on food was Rs.11.49 and Rs.64 for participant and non-participant tribal farmers respectively. The expense on cereals accounted for 69 per cent of the total household consumption expenditure. The diet contained very little protein and milk. Intoxicants formed a major part of household consumption. The expense on food of the Santhals, for example accounted for about 63 per cent of the total household expenditure. The expenditure on non-food items (such as fuel and light, clothing, intoxicants, medical care, education, and even repayment of loans) accounted for 37 per cent of their income. Per capita expenditure on intoxicants was quite high among the tribals but the non tribals spent that much amount on education.

The total amount spent on food did not increase even with an increase in the total family income. This is a typical feature of the people surviving at the subsistence levels. Their income is so low that they got to spend a major part of their very meagre earning on the minimum necessities like food but they do not also want to spend a paisa extra on those unavoidables if they are in a position to do so. They are so miserably deprived of everything that can add a little spice to their life that they would not like to deny themselves of the slightest opportunity to find some enjoyment in their life. They are not able to realize that health, nutrition or investment on land or any other means of livelihood can help them in the long run and to higher income. It is not possible for the "have-nots" to understand what they can have; how can they have a vision of the future when they do not have a future?

Indebtedness affected nearly 38 per cent and 34 per cent of the participant and non-participant farmers respectively, and the amount borrowed is much higher by the participant farmers. They borrowed from Blocs, Co-operatives and the banks, (mostly from banks). Though higher, the loans (taken by the participant farmers) are mainly for productive purposes, i.e. for cultivation, fertilizers, pump sets and drought cattle; the non-participant farmers incurred loans, on the contrary, mainly for consumption, including the observance of the customs and rituals. There are large-scale transfer of lands from tribals to the non-tribals (dikus) as a result of this indebtedness. That serves that as the most unavoidable condition for migration. Indeleted ness is the result of bypassing state laws framed against the alienation of tribal lands. Notice the hypocrisy on the part of our government. Laws are geared towards social welfare or the good of the common people but the developmental plans and market forces act as the worst possible hurdles to true development. They are against the tribals or any other marginlised section of our society. Established tribal scholar Sachhidanand's study (of 1969) of the political institutions of Chhotanagpur indicates that the Rajah, though receiving "chanda" or tribute from the different village communities, was the leader of the people, and not the owner of their lands. The entry of colonialism into the tribal regions of India (through the various forms) broke the 'communal' mode of production; and hence, the emergence of the private right on land. The institution of moneylenders has to be uprooted; the co-operatives and banking systems have to be strengthened and made consumer - friendly. If indebtedness is controlled and productive pattern is improved, migration to towns and cities and to far-off places will be controlled, if not stopped.

a) Poverty

There are two broad concepts of poverty - relative poverty and absolute poverty. The former is measured in terms of inequality in the distribution of income. In developing countries where incomes are low, absolute poverty is generally reflected in the inadequacy of food intake and the consequent undernourishment on a mass scale; the indices include clothing, housing, fuel, lighting, education and health. The poverty-line is mostly drawn in the light of the socially accepted minimum standard of Living. A "poor" in USA may have a higher income than an average incomed person in India. The main components recommended by the Report of the Committee on International Definition and Measurement of Standard of living (UN, 1959) are i) food and nutrition, ii) health, iii) condition of work, iv) education, including literacy and skills, v) Employment situations, vi) Savings and vii) human freedom. Another way of enumerating these factors was by Ganguli and Gupta in 1976. The eight components, according to them were i) nutrition, ii) housing, iii) medical care, iv) education, v) clothing, vi) leisure, vii) security and viii) environment. What affects the life, livelihood and the psyche of the tribals most are the last three components - particularly the last two. With the continuous depletion of the most important means of livelihood for these indigenous people, i.e with the constant degradation of environment, they are losing the sense of security about their life and livelihood; and this is vital for anybody in order to live and find some meaning in living. Equally vital for the tribals are dance, music and other cultural activities. They cannot, unlike the "mainstream" urban people, live in a situation of constant stress and strain (which work in a modern industrialized society, 'offers) Leisure and entertainment are as vital for their living as land, forest, food and shelter are.

The Bruntland Commission Report (1987) says, "poverty is both a cause and effect of environmental degradation"... these two formed a vicious circle. The reasons for degradation were mostly attributed to the unwise management of lands - such as, over-application of chemical fertilizers, waterlogging due to over-irrigation, over-grazing of common lands and, of course, deforestation. So, naturally, women, as family's food and health managers, were the worst sufferers. There was extra load of work as well as the extra burden of mal-nutrition, since women in very poor families survive on left-overs and less the available quantity of food for the family less or nothing will be the amount of the left-overs.

Advanced technology also affected the women farmers badly. In the Nalgonda district of Andhra Pradesh, for example, contribution of women to agricultural production was 80%. But that advantageous position got eroded and erased with the advent of the Green Revolution. Women were forced to become labourers *only* and that too, at a much lower wage. Centre for Science and Environment (New Delhi) had calculated in 1985 that the number of women-cultivators had decreased from 18.4 million to 15.2 million (1951-81), while the number of women-labourers has increased from 15.2 million to 20.95 million. Capitalism claims to have liberated men and women from the shackles of feudal hierarchy and oppression and to have given economic rights to the individuals. But it has actually created a powerful class barrier, by which the "haves" go on having more and more and the "have-nots' continue to have nothing at all. Women are the "have-nots" among the have-nots. So, they get worse-off under the capitalist mode of production.

As a result of environmental degradation and adoption of the latest technologies, and with no sensitization to human and gender problems, women's workload and drudgery have gone up. The economic value of her work as well as her worth in the family have gone down in that proportion since she is, now, able to provide less to her family (as a result of developments beyond her control.) She appears to be contributing less to the family income and productivity because the opportunities to do so are critically reduced. According to Vandana Shiva ("Staying Alive: Women, Ecology and

Survival in India"), ecological destruction and the consequent marginalisation of women in the Third World have been the inevitable results of the Western patriarchal development pattern copied by these countries. (It is important to note, here, that the rich upper-class women, who do not interact with the natural resources for their survival, do not reflect any concern either for women or for the environment).

A six-day seminar organized in 1980 by the Ministry of Agriculture, Government of India, stressed upon involving women in the social forestry programmes, because women are both "the preservers and consumers of the forests and the forest-products". A strong lobby argues that the failures of the developmental programmes are (i) due to non-participation of women and (ii) because local needs and priorities are not taken into consideration.

It has been observed earlier that the quantity of land available, or left for the original owners by the outsider mercantile / industrial enterprises (dikus), is miserably insufficient to cover the need of a family. Cultivable plots in Chhotanagpur have, for years, been subject to fragmentation. Each generation divides and sub-divides the plot, thus rendering it poor in productivity and therefore, uneconomical. Land the provider, now turns out to be a burden. In almost all the fields only one crop is grown and land is kept fallow for the remaining part of the year. People do not have any idea about rotation of crops. Most of them are subsistence farmers growing food-crops only. The idea of taking to cash-crop is considered novel. Besides, what will these simple people do with cash-crops till they have an idea of the market and how it operates? They will suffer a much higher loss and deprivation if they try to enter the market without the necessary knowledge, training and experience.

The education that has been available to them is not enough to ensure a government or a white-collar job; they also lack in the smartness and confidence—the real forte of the middle and the upper class/caste. Even free education (particularly for the Christians) and job reservation(though it is partial and erratic) could not free themselves of this shortcoming. Interaction with the non-tribals or the so-called "mainstream" did contribute, to a certain extent, towards the process of education and confidence-building (of the tribals). The speed of this process has been low and the ultimate success, too, was low.

Educational Status of the Tribal and the Non-Tribal Working Women

	Tribal %	Non-Tribal %
Matriculation	22.2	—
Intermediate	37.7	7.6
Bachelors	31.6	47.1
Masters	6.6	38.04
Doctorate	2.2	6.6

Source: Bulletin of Bihar Tribal Welfare Research Institute, Ranchi, January 1993.

As such, non-agricultural labour is the only alternative left for these people. Even this degraded job is not easily available—such is the extent of human devaluation caused by poverty, which, in turn, is caused by ecological devastation! So, the second alternative is to migrate. The women, particularly those who are young and educated, are keener on migration because they get lower than the already low wage these thoroughly exploited section of our society get. This kind of abominably low and discriminatory wage-rate, undoubtedly, goes against the word and spirit of our Constitution. The eagerness to migrate to urban areas for a better standard of living is a strong desire that creates subconscious jealousy with the brethren settled already in towns and cities. Nevertheless it is the same "biradari" (clan) or the village friends and acquaintances which help them to migrate and find a job.

B

One of the most significant consequences of the changing socio-economic conditions in a growing industrial city like Ranchi (the tribals, under our study, are more or less concentrated in this area) during the past few decades is the phenomenon of women coming out of their seclusion and entering into vocation which offers them relatively more money and less of back-breaking work. Spread of education and lure of "modern" life have made women realize the importance of economic independence; this enables her to gain independent social status, because now she is doing work other than her own household chores - the work which is always, in all societies and in all social strata, unpaid, unrecognized and, therefore, not valued. In addition to the desire of establishing her own identity, a woman-whether poor or from the middle-class, whether tribal or non-tribal— today earns to contribute towards the family income, or to utilize her leisure time in educational pursuits. Besides, material philosophy of life, i.e. to earn and acquire more and more, is taking the place of the old philosophy of *Contentment* with whatever is *ordained* or *given by God*.

In general, an educated, un-married daughter or sister bringing money home is welcome - though, in the process, these girls are confronted with complex social situations which affect their future lives (may be adversely). They can be categorized as women

1) Who work out of economic necessity,
2) Desirous of economic independence and individual social identity.

3) Waiting for marriage (due to family or dowry problems)

4) Whose educational status has proved to be an obstacle to getting a life-partner

5) Who have preferred professional career to marriage

Job Motivation of Unmarried Tribal and Non-Tribal Working Women

Motivation	Tribal %	Non-Tribal %
1. Economic Necessity	33.3	26.6
2. Economic Independence and individualism	16.6	20.0 3.
Waiting for marriage (family/ dowry problem)	—	30.0
4. Education-obstacle in marriage	50.0	23.5

Source: Bulletin of Bihar Tribal Welfare Research Institute, Ranchi, January 1993.

Tribal women, in general, display a better sense of self-respect and courage. The non-tribals, in general as a contrast, continue to bear,in silence, pain and misery inflicted by their husbands or the patriarchal system. The tribal women do not in general, give up job to oblige or please their husbands. If necessary, they get separated from their husbands, continue with their jobs and look after their children (divorce is not all that common).

b) Role of Education

Education seems to be the most significant contributing factor to the promotion of such a psyche, but it contributes to some unwelcome developments also. Education, while giving self-confidence and a sense of dignity, takes away spontaneity and the immense ability to be content with very little, or whatever little Nature offers. Some of the unwelcome impacts of education on a group ,who have been traditionally denied of its benefits, are the following:

a) the desire to improve the standard of living beyond means is, naturally, causing frustration; they have the qualifications but not yet the opportunities because of the age-old system of social discrimination

b) the joint family or community system, which, more often than not, acts as a cushioning to the day-to-day financial and inter-personal tension problems, is cracking up due to the strong feeling of individualism, necessarily created by money-economy and a strong sense of private/individual property.

c) marital adjustments are becoming more and more difficult, as educated wives cannot be easily subjugated or dictated to;they have the confidence to earn and support themselves in case they have to leave home for the sake of freedom.

d) inter-tribal and extra-tribal marriages are becoming more and more common;

e) the tribals are looking forward to towns and cities to satisfy their economic needs (which now include fashion and luxury items); traditional handicrafts - an important means of livelihood - are getting adversely affected; migration to urban areas has become a craze;

Those who manage to get higher education and/or a good job develop a commercial/competitive attitude instead of the co-operative attitude (which was typical with tribal mental build up) and tend to look down upon their own brethren. The tradition of ceremonial friendship, viz: "Sangi" and "Sahiya" is gradually disappearing; socio-economic status, rather social status due to high level of education and economic upliftment is, now, becoming the prime consideration in friendship.

f) To sum up, we can say the new traits of material culture are developing in contrast to the basically non-material traditional culture. This is alienating the tribals from their cultural heritage and identity. The leaders observed, "inspite of we having a culture and civilization of our own,we are losing our identity, because education is imparted through the medium of Hindi or English and not through our own language.The curriculum also does not suit our requirement". The subjects of study,the syllabi,the language and the emphasis—all are dictated and controlled by the highly educated traditional middle-class,aspiring to be upper class.

The tribal, who lives on a subsistence economy, perceives land primarily as a source of survival. For the higher class non-tribal, on the contrary, land is the primary source of power and control understood as "the ability to do things to others which you do not expect they can do unto you" (Philip Viegas in "National Development and Tribal Deprivation" by W. Fernandes (ed.) The privileged tribals (with higher education and highly paid jobs) have, unfortunately, started emulating this society.

c) Egalitarian Society

It is widely known that the tribals have an egalitarian social structure (the concepts of caste and class are absent) based on community living and an in-built system of reciprocity. This pattern did not undergo much change notwithstanding feudal and colonial exploitation over a long period of time. Even the non-tribals, who migrated to and settled in the tribal areas, have, by and large, adopted the egalitarian practices. But gross economic discrimination against women farm labourers is pronounced all the same. The socio-cultural laws are highly discriminatory against women in respect of the distribution of economic work and economic returns. The women have to perform the monotonous work of transplanting, weeding and harvesting but the right over the produce is that of the male members of the society. However, unlike the non tribal women, the tribal women have some control over some forest and minor agricultural products.

In many parts of Africa, women are more closely tied to the resources in their environment than men are. Yet this link has not often been noted, even by environmentalists. "Women use the environment. In many parts of Africa, it is their traditional role to collect firewood. They also have knowledge about medicinal plants and building materials," explains Rose Marie Odiachi of the Commonwealth Secretariat's Management Training Service Division. The major share of agricultural work is done by women in many countries of the world. To highlight this link between gender and environment, a workshop was held in Kampala, Uganda last year. The workshop recognised the vital role that women play in the conservation of environment and affirmed the need for full participation of women at all levels of policy-making and implementation.

Forest based tribal economy was women-centered. Food, fuel, medicine, housing material, etc. were made from forest produce by tribal women. Women contributed more than men in almost all activities like clearing, sowing, weeding, harvesting, etc. Extensive felling of trees has forced the tribal women to walk longer distances in search of forest products. They fall a victim to malnutrition, TB, etc. due to the over-strain, inadequate food intake and destruction of traditional medicinal herbs. Compared to their non-tribal counterparts, the tribal women - particularly the Christians - are educated, but the level of their education and vocational skill is low when compared to their men.

Men, in general, are found spending their time and money in hunting, drinking, gambling and merry making. So, for all practical purposes, a tribal household is run by the females, who are economically deprived due to the gender bias in both mainstream and tribal societies. No investment on or improvement of land is possible since those who slog on land have neither the right to ownership nor the right to plough. A tribal family,thus, gets badly trapped in the vicious circle of poverty - created by the gender bias, discriminatory laws and the so called "developmental process". It may be possible that when the female farm labourers get alternative jobs and income-earning opportunities, their supply curve and wage-rate will move upwards. This will also result in the increase of male participation in agricultural operations and improvement in the economic position of tribal families. This may even help in the removal of stagnation in the tribal economy. In the long run, this may even contribute to the empowerment of the tribal women! But in reality, the supply and demand conditions of women labourers are such that women find it difficult to get alternative or more work.

Migration, normally, is regarded as an economic phenomenon. Economic factors definitely are the prime factors, but political, social and geographic factors also cause migration. Migration can be both voluntary and involuntary. In our study we shall find that the migration of young Munda, Oraon and Santhal girls to a metropolis like Delhi started out of economic compulsion (i.e. involuntarily); but over a period of time, as the flow of migrants continued and increased, it appeared to be semi-voluntary. The girls who found employment as domestic workers (through the assistance of DDWWF or even otherwise) found life and work easy with a reasonably good income. They had enough to enjoy even after sending money home. Thus they made their family and themselves -both happy. This is one of the many reasons why more young women migrate than men. Besides, men stay back to cultivate whatever little land the family is left with. Men do not also get comfortable jobs like domestic work; they usually end up in construction sites where they are badly exploited Very often the migrations are seasonal, i.e. during the lean period in agricultural activities (may be, in December after harvesting upto the beginning of Monsoon). The usual tactics of the contractors are - first, not to let the tribals get hired, so that they have no choice but to offer to work at a reduced rate. The non-tribal workers fight with them for being a cause to the reduction in the rate and they ,naturally,have a greater say as they belong to the class-group which wields power—not only in social decisions but also in political decisions.The tribals are in a much disadvantaged position than even the 'Harijans', since the latter are covered by a"sympathy-wave"pervading,in a diffused manner though,in the Indian polity due to Mahatma Gandhi and his ism. To avoid trouble the contractors get rid of tribal workers. So, the tribals are kept unemployed for as long as possible and their struggle for survival becomes harder and harder. The contractors also impose arbitrary age-limit on the tribal workers to make the prohibition appear legal and non-discriminatory.

The urban population of the Mundas is quite high. About 42% of the Oraons are urban-dwellers. A Christian Oraon woman, for example, says, "our society is changing fast mainly due to changing economic relations. Formerly women used to help men in the fields, but now every woman can earn something for her family. Unless we have sufficient money, we shall not be able to have the amenities of modern life. Now, we cannot do without lanterns; some of us are attracted towards fine saris. Such needs and desires compel us to supplement income of our husbands. Whenever I go to Ranchi, I go to pictures. As a matter of fact, I love to go to pictures."

d) Effects of Development

"Development", as such, is not a disrupting or destructive phenomenon. It is the planners, the governments and the power-wielders in the society who, by their lust for money and power, lack of imagination and knowledge about the" other" and hostility to those who are so different from them (for example, the indigenous people), make things difficult both for themselves and the tribals.

S.Narayan and Vinod Kumar, in their article "Obstacles to Tribal Development" noted that the failure to improve the lots of the tribals (in the tribal areas), had been the result of complex interplay of economic and political forces and many maladies in the administrative machinery. The disparities in the levels of living of the tribals is well discernible in terms of unequal distribution of household productive assets (mainly land and livestock), lack of availability of modern productive techniques, low per capita income, low per capita consumption, absence of market and marketing facilities, lack of subsidiary occupation and other socio-cultural inequalities. Lands, even under settled farming, are poor in quality and the use of fertilizers, improved seeds, pesticides and modern agricultural implements, etc. is seldom evident among the tribals.The tribal areas are hardly ever covered by any of the cooperative banks or societies or government welfare network. There are politicians clamouring for the economically depressed section of their constituencies,a thousand and one NGOS are highlighting their plight, but they are like aliens in the country they originally belonged to. To add to their misery, the tribal cultivators regularly took loans by mortgaging their lands to the money-lenders. Productivity being low, they could seldom get their lands released. Besides, their land holdings were fragmented and became of small, unproductive sizes. It was basically subsistence farming and cash-crops figured rarely in their cropping pattern. Workforce participation rate (outside agriculture)among the tribals is higher when compared to the general population. Conditions of work and the level of remuneration being highly unsatisfactory, this trend heightens the poverty and socio-economic exploitation of the scheduled tribes, as well as of the scheduled castes. In fact majority of the new employment opportunities for these people in the weaker section of the society should have been in agriculture, agro-based industries, cottage industries and forestry, etc.

The money they get as compensation is hardly ever invested in any productive venture. They neither have the idea, nor the experience, nor the training or guidance for this kind of activity. They are born and brought up in the forest and for the forest ; they have a deep inborn knowledge about how to conserve what they are given by their mother viz: the Nature, but they do not know how to bring about changes or to improve upon. They can truthfully fulfil only what mother Nature expects them to do. So, the money, which is meant to be an alternative source of income for livelihood (when their lands are taken away for "developmental projects"), is usually squandered away. They find it as something extra, a bonus,as if. Thus, they slip more and more down into poverty,caused artificially because Nature's egalitarian laws, meant to maintain a perfect equilibrium,are broken by a society that thrives on insurmountable division between man and man as well as between man and woman. Finally, they are uprooted from their soil, from their home and hearth. They are left with no other choice but to migrate in search of livelihood, though that too, becomes like running towards a mirage.

We must, however, keep in mind that tribal land

dispossession is not altogether a new phenomenon.What we call "civilization" was the most ancient and original agent of the alienation and dispossession of the adivasis;there always has been a strife between tradition and change or the new order.The Aryans dispossessed the Dravidians,the Red Indians were dispossessed by the West European colonialists,the Maoris by the deported convicts from the industrialized Europe (to quote a few) and Feudalism by Capitalism. The adivasis got dispossessed even by the petty traders and factory owners who cheated the simple minded tribals of their lands and thus made them subservient.

Land alienation is believed, by many scholars, to be the result of several factors like agricultural capitalism, social formation, modernization and even land legislations. J.P. Mencher, in his article called "Problems in Analyzing Rural class Structure" (EPW), has pointed out that most of the studies call for a critical examination of the legislations as they, ultimately, benefit only the rich farmers. Marx refers to the alienated as "estranged labour". Under certain circumstances or in certain societies the conditions imposed on man are such that he becomes a stranger to himself, as he is *no longer able to recognize himself in his activity or in his productive capacity* (Raymond Aron, "Main Currents in Sociological Thought"). In Marxian perspective, alienation is, at once, a historical, moral and sociological critique of the present socio-economic order, the root of all alienation is, though, economic alienation. Strengthened property relations strengthens the process of alienation. Tribals, that is why, lost control over what they created over ages; they, now, work as landless labour on the same land which were, earlier, under their possession. There is a general lack of purpose and a destructive feeling of insecurity among them. They feel socially marginalised, politically powerless and even culturally peripheral. This happens specially whenever there is a low level of literacy and job-opportunities among them.

(May be it is worthwhile reminding ourselves, at this juncture, that the tribal socio-economic structure is totally framed by their deep and incorruptible belief in community-ownership and community-management of property. We very well know that their dances and songs and all cultural and religious activities are characterized by community participation; their life-style is the best example of individuals living in perfect harmony, maintaining perfect equilibrium in Nature).

Many studies have indicated that the tribal women work more than their male counterparts. Women put in 180 person-days, whereas men put in only 100, inspite of relatively egalitarian pattern of the tribal society. Women's economic contribution to the family is also greater than in a caste society. Women are more particular about environmental conservation since they are the primary providers of food, firewood, fodder, water, herbal medicines and all that one can possibly get from the forest. Notwithstanding the receding forests and therefore, the receding benefits from the forests, the women remain primarily responsible for whatever the adivasis are accustomed to getting from the forest—the only source of livelihood they know of. They, like the women in any other society, are more conscious of their identity and their tradition. But (our study will show later) young tribal women, when they migrate to urban centres—however distant that place may be geographically and culturally—adjust and adapt better. They have a strong motivation for being accepted as part of the mainstream. They are pragmatic and have a powerful urge for survival; they adjust well with what ever the situation demands.

The worst problem that the tribals face is that not

only they possess inadequate land for cultivation, they are unskilled. Even unskilled labour is often brought from outside the tribal area due to the reasons discussed earlier. Besides, it is always easier to put pressure on labour from outside the region, threaten them and even convert them into bonded labourers, since they have no roots and no possible support from their own people. When local labour is recruited, it is only due to the possibility of offering them low wages.

Dams are the biggest agents of displacement, joined by mines, industries and other "development" projects. These are mostly situated in tribal areas; so a large chunk viz: 7.5 percent of the country's population (this is the total tribal population in our country) get continuously displaced from their land, livelihood and socio-cultural roots. As mentioned earlier, women become the worst sufferers, because in the traditional division of work, it is the woman's duty to make provisions for the basic necessities like food, fuel and water. So, they migrate in search of livelihood. The level and the extent of literacy amongst them is very low, opportunities for gainful employment is limited. The Christians are better off though; the missionaries take charge of their education and skill-development and, in quite a few cases, give them the necessary confidence.

5

Change in Life-Style and Occupational Structure

The most obvious impact of migration has been an inclination, on the part of the migrant women, to live in the urban areas in order to enjoy the comforts and the amenities of city life and also to look for regular permanent jobs.

Winick's dictionary of anthropology defines tribe as a "social group usually with a definite area, dialect, cultural homogeneity and a unifying social organization." In 1951, Tribal Welfare Committee consisting of anthropologists, administrators and social workers met in Indian Conference of Social Work (at Calcutta) and recommended the following structure of classification:

1) Tribal communities who are still confined to the original forest habitats and follow the traditional pattern of life and livelihood.
2) Communities, who have more or less settled down in non-forest rural areas and have taken to agriculture and allied occupations.

3) Those who have migrated to urban and semi-urban areas, are engaged in modern industries and vocations and have adopted modern cultural traits.

4) Those who are totally assimilated to non-tribal Indian population.

Ray Burman, an authority on tribal problems, observed—"in many parts of our country, including Chhotanagpur, the primitive remained primitive for a long time.......it was a part of the design of things on the subcontinent. Persistence of primitives, in some parts of the country, allowed a particular pattern of political and social organization to flourish." This, definitely, was in the vested interest of the empowered section who call themselves the "mainstream" (as distinguished from the "primitive", "indigenous", and "tribal").

In India's post-independence period, while vestiges of feudal mode of production continue, capitalist mode of production is rapidly taking over. Indigenous entrepreneurship was lagging behind in these areas and in these cultures mainly because of the persistence of social values not conducive to the accumulation of surplus or any type of wealth. Productive forces in these areas have been, to a considerable extent, harnessed mainly to serve the needs of the "national" market (implying that tribal economy is not a part of the national economy), thus causing great strains of adjustment to the indigenous peoples of the region.

Chhotanagpur is the richest mineral belt in India. It contains world's largest reserve of mica and substantial quantities of iron-ore, coal, copper, bauxite, limestone. Iron-ore had become technologically and socially meaningful to the primitive smelters, but exploitation of other minerals and forest products on any significant scale started only during the colonial period. The nature of terrain should have allowed the people to live in comparative isolation, but the richness and the diversity of the resources invited "dikus" (outsiders) and eco-inimical exploitation of both natural and human resources. Thus, there is conflicting socio-economic interests existing among the post-primitive indigenous inhabitants and the immigrant settlers with commercial goals. Commercialization of the tribal economy naturally influenced the tribal pattern of life and set of values.They started becoming envious and jealous of those who have hit success by migrating to the urban areas, adopting urban life-style and even imbibing urban values. Such "uprooted" tribals served as their models, as if.

a) Exploitation of Women

Though the work participation rate among tribal women has been increasing over a period of time (1971-91), it is lesser than that for the tribal males, but higher than that for the general female population.

Though an overwhelming majority of tribal men (85%) and women (91%) were involved in agriculture, there are more cultivators amongst men while more tribal women were only agricultural labourers. Women and children are almost exclusively involved in collection of minor forest produce, its storage, processing and marketing. Collection of fuel-wood has become more difficult since one has to walk miles due to receding forests. Less fuelwood and less forest products mean less income and lesser nutrition.

This discrimination in the so called egalitarian tribal society places relatively more money and time in the hands of the tribal male; it also leads to idleness and alcoholism on the part of the tribal male and thus causes wastage of money and labour power. They are left with hardly any amount to invest on agriculture for its productivity raising. At the most, they work enough to earn enough for the working capital requirements of their fields.

Other negative effects of "development" programmes are

1) work load on women has increased; they have become pathetic victims of physical and mental strain, less family-income and less nutrition.

2) with modern agricultural implements and modern methods of cultivation, unemployment of women in agriculture has gone up. (since they lack skill and technical training) They are,in fact, not allowed to have access to trainning and skill development. Whatever little a poor family can afford to spend on skill-development it does on the male members only. So, the women are left with no option but to migrate as labourers.

3) receding forests and forest laws like 'trees cannot be cut' have drastically minimized the possibility of earning from the sale of useful forest products like resin, gum, medicines. The laws have marginalised these tribal women thoroughly and completely.

Working women, in all social groups, work much harder (almost double) than men; but this is truer in case of tribal women (notwithstanding their comparatively egalitarian society). They are subjected to other forms of exploitation by the non-tribals—

a) they are lower paid than men (usually half)

b) they are, more often than not,sexually exploited, and

c) new strategies have been devised to remove women from work.

To sum up, the status of a tribal woman is characterized by over-work, invasion of sexually exploitative market forces in the tribal economies, illiteracy, sub-human living conditions, high fertility but high malnutrition and the near absence of modern health care and educational facilities.

c) Role of Education

We know that the overwhelming majority of the tribals (under our study) are Christians and the process of conversion to Christianity was facilitated by the programmes for health and education conducted by the Christian missionaries. Let us, now, try to examine how much education has helped the tribals to fight against exploitation. According to Herbert Spencer "the great aim of education is not knowledge but action". Tribals have their own system of education, which could be perceived in the form of many important institutional processes. Education can also prepare them for the discharge of adulthood roles - various roles normally outlined by one's culture. It can help the tribals get "reserved" services in public and private sectors. Yet, the number of people actually literate (education is a far cry) is dismally low. According to 1981 census, only 16.9% tribals were literate, (out of which 26.17 were males and only 7.75% were females). As a comparison, the literacy rates for the total general population and for the male and females, respectively, are 26.20%, 38.11% and 13.62%. Oraons have the highest literacy rate, viz: 12.69% They have also shown inclination towards achieving higher education. In 1981-91, the number of matriculates rose from 4.19% to 8.33% But it is very low among girls. They are encouraged to work at home.

Even after five decades of independence, most of the tribals have been kept far away from the "mainstream". The chief causes of low literacy rate among these tribals are lack of schools and teachers in tribal areas, high drop-out rate, poor and backward tribal economy, child labour and disinclination of parents/guardians towards their children's education. (We have already noted that the tribals had a rich self-sufficient and self-sustaining economy which became" poor' due to modern developmental exploitations. It is also believed that tribal development is hampered by their low level of aspirations.

The economic backwardness and physical distance from the centers of development are responsible for their educational backwardness. The parents find it more lucrative to engage their children, even of school-going age, in some income-generating activities, rather than spend, however little, on their education. They are sent to school so long they do not get an income-generating occupation.

The tribal economy is afflicted by the insoluble problem of acute fragmented holdings. About 15% of the holdings are below 0.5 hectares. It has been found by Bihar Tribal Welfare Research Institute that, on an average 62% of the tribals are engaged in agriculture, 34% in traditional labour and only 4% in service. The educational background of the people under study was as follows in 1989-90.

	Males	**Females**
Illiterate	63.33%	75%
Primary Education	13.33%	10%
Middle Education	13.33%	10%
Matriculation	6.66%	5%
Post-Matric	3.33%	—

According to 1991 census, female literacy in Chhotanagpur is less than half (21.03%) of male literacy (45.52%). The literacy rate of the tribals is lower than that of the Scheduled Castes even, and the literacy rate of the rural tribal female is the lowest. The female literacy rates vary from zero per cent in some tribes to 33.4% (in Khasis and Jaintias of the North-east).

Education has provided them with the closeness to a town and an opportunity to imbibe the characteristics of an urban culture. This is supposed to provide them with increased job-opportunities. But this actually does not happen (or happens in an insignificant proportion) due to the bias against the tribals. They are considered primitive (in a contemptuous sense), uncivilized and even barbarians! The Constitution and the laws are in their own place and they seem to have the least influence on the minds of those who weild power and take decisions.The centuries-old prejudices and practices continue unabated however modern and progressive the society may appear to be. As pressure on land has increased, the tribals are seeking employment as labourers in nearby towns;they are also migrating to far off places in search of some kind of livelihood.

Educational system plays an important role in the training, development and allocation of resources. In a developing country like India it is expected that the educational system will become not only a key mechanism for the economic development of various sections of its people but also a powerful instrument for accelerating the process of social change. (H.Talesra, "Tribal Education"). The contents and orientation of tribal education has to be geared up according to the social conditioning in which the tribals live. The key problem of the tribals of Bihar is to improve their quality of life; it includes housing, sanitation and health-care along with facilities of education.

But how will a mere house or healthy surrounding help if people do not have the basic means for survival i.e. a decent income/livelihood? Are the tribals assured of that? Have they not been systematically robbed or denied of that fundamental human right? Is not the agenda for the rich and the powerful (the upper-caste/upper-class combine) the agenda for the entire nation and are not the government officials and the rich N.G.O.s party to the same vested interest? Any study on the tribals or any other marginalised group in our society needs to answer these questions.

Education has, and can, expose the tribals to the outside world and enable them to attain a higher socio-economic status. "Education is a manifestation of perfection already present in man", said Swami Vivekananda. That is why, "education has to be purposive not only in the overall sense of helping to build up the individual's personality, character and intelligence, but also in terms of his productive capacity and his ability to take his due place in the army of workers who have to fight the battle for economic growth". (Dr. V.K. R.V. Rao, 1966)

d) The Uprisings

Chhotanagpur became the centre of dynamic separatist movements due to a combination of many factors. First, it was the most advanced of the tribal regions with regard to literacy (excluding, of course, the hill tribes of the North East), industrial progress and political consciousness. In fact, the area is a covetable mine of wealth and prosperity due to the easy availability of rich mineral resources. As such, the industrial development and employment opportunities to the inhabitants could have been much more. Secondly, the major tribal communities of India are concentrated in this geographically distinct region. Thirdly, Christianity and the benevolent work of the Christian missionaries, gave the tribals the much-needed confidence and an enlightened attitude. It also introduced and accentuated the notion of private rights on land, a sense of separateness from the rest (or from the "non-enlightened" non-Christians.) The missionaries often combined their proselytizing activities with the spread of education and other welfare measures like medical care, training in crafts, etc. Although conversion to Christianity (or to any other religion) tended to uproot the tribals from their traditional norms and linkages, it also provided a basis for developing a new type of unity due to their accentuated consciousness. It helped them to fight the Hindu-dominated world around with greater confidence.They needed to fight this world because it comprised not only of the numerical majority but also of those who wielded economic and political power because of their privileged position in the society, Fourthly, this area was the field of operation of many interest. The Bengalis formed a sizable professional and land-onwing community, and the Muslims were found to have significant trading and professional interests. The Bengali-Bihari controversy over employment in the late 1930s as well as the Muslim League politics contributed to the intensification of tribal separatist movement.

1938-47 saw the rise of a militant movement under the Adivasi Mahasabha. When Indian National Congress, a body of elites trying to decide the destiny of India (where the overwhelming majority of the people are either "adivasis" or lower castes) swept the polls in 1937 elections, the non-Christian adivasis joined hands with the Christians. The Chhotanagpur Unnati Samaj and other organizations working for the tribals merged to form the Adivasi Mahasabha. Jaipal Singh Munda was the President. In the period between 1949 to 1963, the Adivasi Mahasaba was wound up and Jharkhand Party was formed. The Mundas and the Oraons joined the Sardar Movement (1859-1895), which sought to establish the peasant rights of the tribal people. Within a few years of the establishment of the zamindari system, the merchants,the mahajans and the zamindars amassed large fortunes and reduced the Santals to the status of serfs. Sidhu and Kanhu, the two legendary leaders, preached, "we should pay only eight annas for a buffalo plough and four annas for a bullock plough and if the rulers did not agree, we should start fighting. We should slay all the despeakable "Dikus" and become the rulers ourselves." (Culshaw and Archer, 1945).

The Santal rebellion of 1855-56 preceded the rebellion of the Sepoys (1857) (now described as the First War of Independence). This was a struggle for tribal autonomy from the Dikus and their allies, viz. the British rulers. A section of the Mundas and the Oroans were involved in violent uprisings at Chiri (Ranchi district). A large number of migrant tribals from Chhotanagpur had settled down in Naxalbari (West Bengal), which later became the hotbed of terrorist uprisings. The Birsa Seva Dal, during its militant phase of 1967-69, demanded the creation of a separate state, the expulsion of non-Chhotanagpuris, agrarian reforms and measures against money-lenders. They bind the tribals in perpetual indebtedness- sometimes as bonded labour - and the bulk of them are yet unable to cross the threshold of unskilled labour in mines, factories and plantations. The activities of Birsa Seva Dal, were concentrated in the urban areas of Ranchi and Jamshedpur. The failures of the sporadic militant movements and the firm establishment of the Constitution of India,declaring basic human rights as the Fundamental Rights helped these disgruntled lot to perceive their problems in the right perspective and give a radically new direction to their movement.We can, perhaps, comment, "there was thus a transition from ethnicity to regionalism", with emphasis on the economic factors. (K.S.Singh,"Tribal Movements in India"). The leaders, naturally, came from the higher strata of the tribal societies - the Munda and Manki in the Ho region, the Manjhi and Parganaities in the Santal region and the educated Christians from the Munda and Oraon areas. The Mundas provided the leadership for the students' movement in 1915-20. A regulated supply of adequate money was necessary to sustain such organization and movements. The search for money led to strange alignments with the "dikus", whose interests, in fact, go against those of the adivasis! The non-Bihari dikus had a vested interest in the movement to keep the Bihari dikus away. Political parties, apparently working for the tribals, supported these outsiders because politics is rooted in power and power is rooted in money,the right alignments and the hallowed slogans and promises.

Both the political parties and the dikus , thus, have vested interest in the indefinite and frustrating continuation of this movement; they also want the movement to lose its perspective and the activists to lose their vision and determination so that the region and its people perennially remain disturbed, unsettled and, therefore, disunited. A movement, when successful, may achieve wonders,may change the system radically,but, during its course, is the most unsettling force for a society and its people. The movement loses its momentum and may even get disintegrated if it goes out of its time-frame. The worst victims,then, are the people,themselves for whom and by whom the movement originally started........These hapless people were brutally exposed to supra-ethnic trade-union politics and as the lowest category of industrial workers.

The tribals are ever keen to maintain their social and cultural identity and the loss of that hurts them deeply. This was a significant reason behind most of the rebellions.

"Father of the Earth, ours is the land. Our ancestors left their footprints. In the country reclaimed by us, you made others sit in our property. Our ancient order was wiped out..." Birsaite Song.

The 1971 Census disclosed an alarming state of affairs. The percentage of tribal population in the tribal districts fell sharply - in Ranchi from 61.61 to 58.08, in Singhbhum from 47.31 to 46.12, and in the Santal Parganas from 38.24 to 36.22 (in one decade)

6

Planning for Tribal Development

The tribals occupy a unique position in Indian culture with their diverse and colourful cultural traditions. Yet they are the last - even after the scheduled castes - among the beneficiaries of progress. K.S. Singh, in his book - 'Tribal Movements in India', remarks, "A tribe in India is an administrative concept which means the communities scheduled as tribes under the Indian Constitution." As it is a legal concept, *a tribe can be descheduled at the will of the majority in the parliament* within the Constitutional provision, and thereby, be denied of their rights at any time.

From the anthropological point of view, a tribe is 'an ideal state as self-contained unit'. It constitutes a society in itself. Anthropologist, Nadeal, defines a society in this way: "Societies are made up of people, societies have boundaries, people either belonging to them or not, and people belonging to a society in virtue of rules under which they stand and which impose on them regular, determinate ways of acting towards and in regard to one another" The working definition of the "Indigenous Peoples", adopted by the United Nations is - "Indigenous Communities, peoples and nations are those which having a historical continuity with pre-invasion, pre-colonial societies that developed in their territories, consider themselves distinct from other sectors of societies now prevailing in those territories or parts of them. They form at present non-dominant sectors of society and are determined to preserve, develop and transmit to future generations their anscestral territories and their ethnic identity as the basis of their continued existence as people in accordance with their own cultural patterns, social institutions and legal system." Their society is characterized by the fact of being

(1) egalitarian

(2) co-operative, not competitive

(3) group-participation - not individual performance (e.g. songs and dances)

(4) consensus-based

(5) intimate and living relation with nature

(6) strong conviction in 'the society or community before the individual' and

(7) a healthy and uninhibited approach to sex.

But now, due to the age-old policies of unequal development and exploitation, the tribals are known for their poor living conditions, high rate of illiteracy, disease and mortality, less social and political awareness and unemployment even in the primary sector. About 85 per cent was engaged in agriculture (1981) with per capita cultivated land of 0.68 acre against a State average of 0.36 acres. Yet, their per capita income was only Rs.148/- against all India figure of Rs.421/-. This reflects the defects in the development strategies planned/implemented for tribal regions. All the Constitutional provisions and special welfare measures failed to achieve the desired goal. So, the tribal population, in general, feel alienated from the mainstream of social and economic developments. They are alienated, as the developmental activities, invariably, take away their wealth and benefit those who contribute nothing. These indigenous people,till now, have got nothing in return of everything that they are continuously made to give up. The resultant discontent is expressed in various forms of political agitations - quite often supported even by the mainstream parties. (The reasons for this have been discussed earlier.)

From time to time, scholars like Majumdar, Dubey, Bose, Chattopadhayay and Vidyarthi suggested ways and means to ameliorate the dismal socio-economic conditions of the tribals. Nehru, the first Prime Minister of India, had suggested, very correctly, that the tribals should be helped to develop "along the lines of their own genius". While planning tribal development, their economy and socio-cultural characteristics in relation to their habitat should be kept in mind. Uncontrolled and illicit felling of trees, over-grazing and burying (of the dead) have to be banned. Suitable wasteland has to be drawn into forest estate. Conservation of soil and water, needless to mention, is a must. Where agriculture is not sufficiently productive to support the farmers, it is necessary to encourage the formation of co-operatives for dairy or poultry-farming. The scope of their income can be widened through the wise exploitation of forest and mineral resources and the establishment of the small scale industries. (It is everybody's knowledge that the area under our study is the richest in India in mineral resources.) Industries based on herbs and medicinal plants can be very meaningful for the area and its inhabitants; above all, the production and marketing should be totally managed by the local people, supported— financially and technologically— by the local government. The "dikus" should never get a chance to exploit the innocent tribals. The long term objectives of planning for the tribals have to be (1) to narrow down the gaps between the levels of development of tribal and other areas and thus, (2) to improve their quality of life and life-supporting opportunities.

The Report of the Scheduled Areas and Scheduled Tribes Commission (1961), under the chairmanship of U.N. Dhebar, had spelt out the following guiding principles for tribal development.

(1) The tribal should be made to feel that his/her way of life, beliefs and customs will not be tampered with.

(2) He/She should feel safe about his/her land-right.

(3) His/Her rights over forest and forest products should be equally safe.

(4) He/She should be made to understand, in a slow and friendly manner and not forced to accept, that changes are inevitable and no real development is possible without some changes in the socio-economic set-up. He/She should be able to perceive the government and the mainstream society as his/her friend and benefactor. For this to happen the unavoidable changes got to be accompanied by schemes for meaningful rehabilitation, education, training (vocational) and equipments.

(5) Till this actually happens, a tribal should not be disturbed from the mooring of his agriculture-cum-forest economy.

(6) Thorough research and sympathetic study are a must as a base for all benevolent developmental activities to begin.

A Naga girl had once observed, "when my friends ask me why do you not accept that you are an Indian, I answer, are you prepared to accept us as Indians"? She has posed a crucial question. the responsibility of nation-building cannot be thrust on any particular ethnic identity in isolation. It is the responsibility of all. If the social change of the

Nagas is to be oriented towards the rest of the country, the Bengalis, the Punjabis, the Tamils, the Telugus have also to be prepared to incorporate in their culture and way of life, streaks of Naga culture and way of life. (Roy Burman, 1988).

Here are a few responses of the participants of the National Workshop on the Rehabilitation Policy (February, 1995) to the Draft Rehabilitation Policy of the Government of India.

(1) For any policy to have teeth it must be translated into a legally justifiable document, i.e. a law.

(2) The affected population must have a right to participate in all processes which determine and affect their future.

(3) The affected people were not involved by the Government in the discussions leading to the draft policy. How can anybodyelse know what and how much they have lost,and what and how much they should get as a compensation. Their democratic right is abrogated by this secrecy.

(4) The Draft Policy is gender-blind. It restricts the family to the household, with the male as the head and the deciding agent for compensation and rehabilitation.

(5) Any such policy should recognize the historically established rights of the people over their resources, v.i.z.land, Nature's bounty and traditional knowledge.

(6) The Policy, unfortunately, ignores the social and psychological trauma connected with displacement. Attitudes towards the movements and the displaced persons would have been pragmatic and sympathetic, otherwise.

(7) The policy must recognize that ecological and

> environmental destructions are neither unavoidable nor irreversible. In fact, in the long run, these work against development, itself. By destroying Nature we destroy the resources and the potentials that can sustain the development, itself.

The attitude of the development planners and executors can be displayed thus -

"Excuse me, please vacate your house.

We need it for national prosperity.

No, no, we are not joking. You don't know what to do with your house.

You really must be a fool to want to live in it

Or to grow flowers in the backyard.

We need it for National Prosperity.

What is National Prosperity, you ask?

Come on -

"National" means all of us; we will all be prosperous, you see.

Of course, you will also get a part of it.

We will pull down your house and set up a factory there.

Surely, we will give you a reasonable price for it, er...say, Rs.3,000?

And, then, do you want a job?

....Oh, you are too old!

Then, how about your son?

He is too young.

May be your brother?

What do you mean what kind of a job?

Why, the very best he could ask for.

While we are pulling down your house, he can be a watchman.

He can even wash cars or grow flowers in one of our houses.

You still not convinced?

....

Now, get the hell out of here. I cannot spend so much time with you.

We have to build the Nation."

Feminist researchers, in the recent past, have exposed a major drawback in the development process in the world today— the explicit and implicit ignoring of the needs of women and a strong androcentric bias which assumes that what is good for men is also good for women, thus amalgamating women's needs with those of men. This bias undermines the potential of women-oriented developments in improving the overall poverty situation. In poor countries this bias has additional significance since it adds to the already great hardships imposed on women by poverty - thus making them victims of the double oppression of poverty and sex-discrimination.

The division of work is heavily loaded against women; tribal women under our study are no exceptions. In addition to an equal share in the production process, she has to take the sole responsibility of household chores, which by itself, is a stupendous task. Child-rearing is also her sole responsibility. Tribal women carrying the child on her back while working in the field, is a common sight. Never, not even as an exception, a tribal man can be seen carrying a child on his back, while working. A study by P.C. Deogharia (published in Social Change, December 1993) points out that "one of the important characteristics about the nature of the tribal women of Chhotanagpur is that women are more involved in all types of work and that is why, the work participation rate is more among women."

All over the Munda land, before the coming of alien zamindars and moneylenders (dikus), (i.e. before the entry of money for the purposes of profit-making and exploitation, or,in other words, for the purposes of denying the real producers of their legitimate share) in the 19th century, the loom of time had woven the tribals and the non-tribals (sadan) into a socially and economically integrated pattern. The latter used to respect the social and economic specialities of the Mundas and, through their operations, imparted a fullness and an economic self-sufficiency to the tribal villages. The tribals, therefore, did not look upon them as aliens, but accepted them as adjuncts of their communal life. This is apparent from the similar pattern of life led by the tribals and the non-tribals. Social occasions like name-giving ceremony, marriage, etc., names of days and months, household utensils, tools, weapons, dress, houses and even the language were common to both (Suresh Singh, 1966). The tribals engage themselves in a variety of occupations such as forestry and food gathering, shifting cultivation, settled agriculture, agricultural labour, animal husbandry, household industry,etc. and various studies tell us about the perfect association between the tribals and the Hindu peasantry. Only after the establishment of industrial complexes in places like Ranchi, Jamshedpur and Rourkela, the tribals have come in contact with a heterogeneous population, which could not understand or adjust to tribal culture and tradition. Therefore the tribals started feeling distant, threatened and alienated. The process of displacement of the indigenous people got rolling at this juncture. History shows that with every jump at civilization we lose much in order to gain some.In fact, as the wheel of "advancement" is rolling ahead humanitarian and communal (the word "communal", here, is used in the sense it is understood in the West) values are giving way to non-personal, individualistic and material objectives. So, these simple, selfless, Nature-and-community-oriented people have no place in this world. Their world has been snatched away from them.

Everywhere in this region there is a network of traditional weekly markets where the tribals interact and communicate with different castes and communities i.e. non tribals. (Surajit Sinha, 1958) These markets are significant for the purposes of information and communication. These were centres for social, religious and political activities. The modern consumerist market etho's has now become a powerful source of change in this region.

B

A social movement is a deliberate collective endeavour to promote change in a certain direction, but by any means not excluding violence, illegality, rebellion or revolution. It must evince a minimal degree of organization - may vary from a loose, informal to a highly institutionalized or bureaucratized form. And, a social movement's commitment to change and the raison d'etre of its organization are founded upon the conscious volition and normative commitment to the movement's aims or beliefs, and active participation of the followers or members (Paul Wilkinson, 1971). According to Cameron, "a social movement occurs when a fairly large number of people get bound together in order to alter or supplant some position of existing culture or social order, or to redistribute the power of control within a society"

The word diku (meaning"outsider", but implying "exploiter") is used for those non-tribals who are economically influential and, quite often, connected to political power. Therefore, they are exploitative. Non-tribal poor (who themselves are exploited by the rich non-tribals) — the blacksmith, the barber, the dom and other low-castes—are not regarded as diku. Interestingly, the Hinduised Mundas do not regard the local Brahmans or Vaishnavs as dikus! Thus we see that there is no generalized bias, amongst the tribals, against the non-tribals and there is no conscious caste or class angle to the fear and hatred. A classless and casteless society, or a society,which is not founded on artificial barriers between man and man and man and woman,but is characterized by freedom of the individual with a strong sense of loyalty to the community,cannot be afflicted by the maladies of shortsighted generalizations and the vested interests of a narrow group that has usurped power.So a non-tribal is considered a diku *only if and when* he exploits.

The tribal society is based, primarily, on amity and understanding and, as we have already noted, the tribals had a perfect relation of amity and understanding with the non-tribals till British colonialism and the present day industrialization and commercialism started exploiting and alienating them. In fact, they have started experiencing a sense of alienation even vis-a-vis their own people who have made it to the higher rung of the mainstream society. These privileged tribals, too, have started feeling distant and different from their own people.

Even before Birsa, the Mundas had taken up arms against the local landlords and the British administration (which had brought about the institutions of landlords/ zamindars) in 1789, 1797 and 1832. Birsa had led the first attack in 1895. The tirade against the dikus was kept alive till Birsa's death. The Mundas saw in Birsa a saviour and a prophet.

The Tana Bhagat movement of the Oraons started in 1913-14 under the leadership of Jatra, and the significant years before that were 1820, 1832, 1890 and 1895-1900. The followers of Jatra became "bhagats" and also started leading ascetic life; they abstained from drinking and meat-eating and stopped believing in witchcraft or more than one God.

"Permanent Settlement" was imposed on the Santal inhabited areas in 1793. The Birsingh movement of 1854 was the first organized revolt against the local landlords. In 1871, Bhagirath led another such uprising. The Bangam movement of 1930 was inspired by Gandhian ideals. These movements served the double purpose, viz. (1) to fight the dikus and also to reform and revitalize their own societies. The process of modernization, rising expectations and the spread of education have helped the emergence of a middle class among the tribals also. This class, in any society, is always most vocal and articulate. The demand for a separate state of Jharkhand is the rallying call to the tribals of different groups to voice their political opinion.

The Chhotanagpur Tenancy Act of 1908 prohibited the transfer of tribal land to non-tribals. The indigenous people get dispossessed of their land by the so-called "legal" method of acquiring land for public purposes. The Act was amended in 1947 to suit the purposes of urbanization and industrialization in the name of development.

As a result, the family-life of the tribals is getting disrupted. They are losing their control over their means of livelihood and are becoming more and more vulnerable to diseases and emotional disorders. Crimes, suicides, delinquency are becoming common among them. They are feeling the deprivation of their sense of personal worth and a devaluation of their social identity. This feeling takes a devastating shape because of the negative attitude and approach of the dominant society towards the tribals culture and socio-economic conditions. To add to their misery, political authorities chosen from the dominant social strata,groups and factions are appointed over them. So, the latter are becoming more and more politically powerless. " They are turned into "free" workers, independent from and deprived of the material means of their own reproduction". (Mathew Areeparampil).

The process of modernization was introduced among the tribal people by the Christian missionaries from Europe with the active support of the British Raj. The missionaries expanded their evangelical, educational, medical and welfare activities; they also managed to secure for their converts basic civic rights and employment in public services. With the tribals who embraced Christianity, religious identity became dominant over their ethnic identity. It gave them a sense of dignity and equality with others(i.e. the non-tribals) belonging to the same religion.

A considerable section among the educated took to non-traditional occupations which could give them good earning. (In the census reports they got entered as Indian Christians and not as tribals). The tribal converts, quite often, consider themselves different from the non-Christians and acquire a sense of superiority. They even start believing that the non-Christians are immoral - that they drink excessively, speak "filthy" language, perform dances mixing freely with the opposite sex and do not even have proper manners or civic sense.

The non-converts saw their own people getting the benefits of development and modernization — particularly jobs and English education- merely due to the virtue of being Christians. This made the Christians relatively smart and sophisticated. The contrast was so glaring that more and more tribals got attracted to this "beneficial/benevolent" religion. The perception of this contrast led to social awakening also. It made them think. They wondered, could they do something to ameliorate their condition without necessarily getting converted to Christianity?

7

Sustainable Development For The Tribals

I

Sustainable development may be defined as the result of successful management of resources for various development processes to satisfy changing human needs. It should also include conserving natural resources as well as maintaining and enhancing the quality of the environment. If poverty is to be eliminated, environmental issues got to be addressed both at micro and macro levels.

A right to development belongs to the so-called third generation of rights, and has received much support, particularly from African nation-states, in international fora. In India, it has been projected less as a right and more as a part of the 'national consensus' on the centralizing, nation-building model of economic and political development. The right of the 'nation' to development is balanced against the right not to be displaced, and a utilitarian calculus of numbers prevails to suggest that the development of all cannot be held at ransom by the emotional attachments to 'backwardness' of a few. This conflict is negotiated very much on the terrain and the terms of the state, backed by international lending agencies.

Indigenous plants and trees provide diverse and nutritious food and are extremely vital during hungry seasons and famines. They can also provide many useful non-food products and sources of income, particularly for women. As they often grow on marginal lands or form part of multi-cropping systems, indigenous plants increases land-use efficiency. Such trees are seldom as "wild" as they are perceived by non- indigenous people; they are often integral parts of indigenous farming systems. They may be protected, managed or even deliberately planted by the farmers.

The alienation of the tribal person from the natural resources by which s/he lives, has a psychological as well as economic impact. Undercutting her psychological dependence on nature - which provides her with food, firewood, medicines, housing materials, and culture - has adverse effects on her health, as some studies of the resettlement experience have shown. It also effects a new, irreversible and yet precarious dependence on agriculture - through labour - as the meagre cash compensation is quickly consumed. The loss of community itself is irreplaceable, and ought to be non-negotiable. The fact that it is neither recompensable, nor brought about after dialogue and consultation, also make it arbitrary and undemocratic. The rights include the right to primary resources such as forests, pastures and water, the right to traditional institutions of self-government, the right to life and existence; and above all, the right to the preservation of their particular cultures and ways of life.

The household environment maintained by women in Sri Lanka, for example, directly or indirectly depend on trees. Women manage trees to obtain food, fodder, fuel, medicinal ingredients, organic residues for enriching soil and materials for fencing, construction, etc. In the area under our study women gather mostly Mohua. Its products, like oil, liquor and dry-fruit, have significant cultural and commercial values. In fact, all over the Third World, there is a special relationship between the women and the trees. Enabling women to derive benefits from tree-resources, e.g. by involving them in the cash-economy of tree- cropping, is clearly a rewarding strategy in tree planting. This is also an essential factor in the conservation of energy and environment.

Everything collected from the forests, except timber, are called "minor forest produce." They are "minor" because they are commercially less valuable and that is why they are relegated the domain of female enterprise. These "minor forest produce" are important raw materials for various industries, like medicine, tanning, food, etc.

Mechanization and industrialization lead to overdrawing of natural wealth and consequential environmental degradation. It throws women out of employment or out of their natural and traditional source of livelihood. Wealth gets concentrated in a few greedy hands and the gap between the rich and the poor gets widened and further widened.

Certain groups in the developing countries (e.g. landlords, entrepreneurs, merchants, military rulers salaried public officials and even trade union leaders), enjoying high income, social status and political power, constitute a small elite ruling class and their principal interest is in the perpetuation of the international capitalist system of inequality and conformity. They, obviously get rewarded by this approach. If development policies, strategies and programmes are oriented towards this goal and shaped by this approach, disadvantaged groups or people get further marginalised. This discrimination is more obvious and blatant in rural and tribal societies, particularly with women. Extensive industrialization and high level of technology ignore the ability and contribution of women and their status goes down further. Industrial societies and regions see greater oppression and violence against women, particularly the rural poor and the tribals; they are forced, by their pauperization, to migrate to industrial and urban centres. Historical study will show that quite a good number of industries, on the contrary, were originally the exclusive domain of women. These were snatched away by men due to the advent of mechanization and automation, since women are not allowed the training and skill associated with it.

Similarly, steady curtailment of the traditional rights of the tribals on forests impaired their economic base and diminished their homoeostatic and natural quality of life. The protective measures for the Scheduled Tribes and the National Forest Policy are not adequate to compensate for the loss. Minor forest produce used to account for 10 to 50 per cent of their income.

Jadugora, the site of India's first and main uranium producing mine is in Singhbhum East district of Jharkhand (Bihar), and lies just 25 kms from the Steel city of Jamshedpur. It is the heart of the Ho and Santal adivasi/ tribal belt. Uranium Corporation of India Ltd. (UCIL), which comes under the Atomic Energy Department of the Government of India, owns and manages three major uranium mines in this area,viz. Jadugora, Batin, and Narwapahar.

Chatijkocha was once a prosperous village; the tribal people of this village had a good yield from their fields that produced crops twice a year, the forest was nearby and villagers enjoyed the bounties of the forest produce. Chatijkocha has a high literacy rate, and is also the home of one of the famous Santal theatre groups, led by a Santal stage artist and script writer, Ishwar Soren.

This Chatijkocha village stood refuge for the displaced adivasi families when they were displaced for the construction of Jadugora Mines and its residential colonies. In 1985 the UCIL management served notice on the villagers of Chatijkocha that they were going to acquire their lands for the third tailing pond. After that nothing much happened. Nine years leter, in 1994, the UCIL Management served another notice to the villagers saying that they have acquired their lands and that they should come to the UCIL Office to collect their compensation, failing which the money would be handed over to the State Treasurer. The villagers refused to accept this meagre compensation and put a set of demands before the UCIL Management this, till date has not been attended to.

On 27th January, 1995 a day after the Republic Day celebrations, the UCIL Management, led by its Chief Managing Director Mr. G.L. Bhasin, the Technical Director Mr. K.K. Berry, the Estate Manager Mr. A. Haquim, the Central Reserve Police Force (CRPF), the Central Industrial Security Force (CISF), the Bihar Police, a set of heavy duty bulldozers and a high- powered diesel- operated shovel, entered Chatijkocha and, without any warning, started bulldozing the houses of the villagers. They came at 11 a.m., at a time when most of the able-bodied villagers were out to work or in the forest and only the invalids and children were at home. Houses that were locked were bulldozed without even caring to inquire if anybody could be in. This demolition squad spread terror to such an extent that the villagers were dumb-struck. Said one villager to me, " it was a one-sided war, similar to the United States trying to bulldoze Iraq".

The question of displacement and land alienation is so acute in Jharkhand, and in Jadugora area in particular, that the people of this area had set up their own displaced persons organization called "Jharkhand Adivasi Vistapit

Berojgar Sangh" (Displaced and Unemployed Union of Tribals of Jharkhand). The office of JAVBS is in Chatijkocha itself. This operation 'Desert Storm' was planned by the Management of UCIL and the District Authorities on a day when they knew that the office-bearers of the JAVBS would be miles away in the District Court to regar to some other case. On the second day,28th January,they shamelessly continued levelling out the village, as men, women and children stood there watching in agony. All they owned and possessed, all their life-sustaining beliefs and belongings were being crushed to dust and pulp.

On 29th January, the third day of operation 'desert storm', they could take it no longer and under the leadership of JABVS, villagers from the surroundings villages came in huge numbers protesting; the women slept before the bulldozers, raising slogans "give us rehabilitation or send us to heaven". Thus, after levelling down houses of over thirty families, levelling down their fields, and desecrating their sacred groves, graveyards and the holy of holies within the hearth of their houses, the 'allied forces' retreated to the comforts of their guest houses. Mission accomplished.

"I am most unhappy that development projects displace tribal people from their habitat, especially as project authorities do not always take care to properly rehabilitate the affected population. But sometimes, there is no alternative and we have to go ahead in the larger interest……." Indira Gandhi

"My dear people, all my brothers and sisters and cousins and grannies. I am talking for my land……. not only my land but your land too. We have to stand up for it. We don't go short of nothing at all. We don't buy. No, we get free what God gives us...The land we have is our forefathers' land ...we cannot give away our land. We don't want jobs. We don't want money. We don't want the

Companies to take our land" - Aboriginal elder of Australia speaking out against the aluminum companies taking his people's land for mining bauxite, (in **'From Massacre to Mining' - Janne Roberts).**

"White people came here a long time ago; took all the furs; trapped all the beaver out: and the otter and the mink, things like that; and they gathered all these things up. They went away and they left us with the bush and the rocks. It wasn't too much later they came back again. They call that logging. Cut down all the trees; white pine, red pine, cut it all down. And they left us on the bare rocks. Then they discovered uranium here. And the old man said, "now the sons-a-bitches are back for the rocks." - Gilbert Oskaboose, Serpent River Band. Canada. (Update Collective, No.84) In the Indian situation, the ruling class are like the Whites.

Development must be redefined as an attack on the chief evils of the world today, viz: malnutrition, disease, illiteracy, slums, unemployment and inequality. Measured in terms of aggregate growth-rate, development has been a great success. But, measured in terms of jobs, justice and the elimination of poverty, it has been a grand failure.

Theoretically, economic growth and the "development" projects benefit the majority of a country's population. As the economy becomes efficient, it is expected to create more jobs and more income. But, in reality, in underdeveloped and developing economies, "developmental" activities create more of inequalities between men and women and between ethnic, caste and regional groups. "Growth" fails to reach certain sections - rather the overwhelming majority of the people. Unable to face the competition with the rich and the privileged, the common people slide more and more down; they remain unable to take advantage of the fresh opportunities generated by the economic change which is prodded by the imperialism of global capitalism.

"Growth" does not necessarily mean greater inequality. Educated and fearless voters can bring in a sensitive, pro-people government and that government (in the true spirit of democracy) can change the definition of "growth" and "development" (the way we have defined above) and make it hundred and one percent pro-people. Growth, thus redefined, can reduce inequality in the long run - as it has happened in the case of Colombia, Indonesia and Malaysia.

We must tackle with a few environmental myths so that the deprived and the dominated are not deprived and dominated further.

MYTH 1 : The poor are destroying the environment

Answer: The poor have the biggest stake in protecting the natural resource base, which provides water, food, fodder and housing free or at a minimal cost. The state, in collusion with big business houses contributes to the damage of the environment. These forces have created major rifts within communities and between people and their natural environments.

MYTH 2: Population growth is responsible for environmental degradation

Answer: Extremes of wealth and poverty, leading to over-consumption by some and the erosion of livelihoods for others, unequal distribution and use of resources and patterns of human settlements, have a stronger relationship to environmental degradation than population size, by itself.

MYTH 3: Structural Adjustment will set right the problems of poverty, employment and environment

Answer: The clash of interests is indicated to be not only between governments and people, but also between governments and major institutions, in collusion with big business, which own and control the major share of the world's resources.

(Environment and Development: Grass Roots Women's Perspectives, prepared by the DAWN group for UNCED 92. The extracts are based on case studies and women's perspectives on the issue).

(From Tribune, Newsletter 40, February 1993)

Women's hard work is linked to low income, poor health and nutrition, low status and no appreciation or recognition of work/contribution to GNP. What would happen if these women were policy-makers and they came up with new policy initiatives like these?

* Vigorous tree-planting programmes
* Credit and loan programmes for women involved in small business-projects, e.g. agriculture, transport, housing, waste-disposal and recycling, marketing, trucking, etc.
* The creation of new programmes for girls in schools to stimulate an interest in technology, and encourage their entry into environmentally-friendly technology fields.
* Trade and market subsidies so that existing and future technologies will be accessible and appropriate for use by women.

(From Tribune, Newsletter 49, February 1993)

Women's hard work could then lead to higher income, better health and a life of fulfilment.

"Women..... defend your land from loggers". "A block of land is a woman's livelihood. If she loses that, she becomes destitute." (Nahau Rooney,Forest Industries Council,Papua New Guinea.) In Papua New Guinea (PNG), many men are working away from their villages, putting women under pressure to defend their land from loggers, i.e. the corporations that cut down trees and truck the logs out for lumber. Women need the forests for firewood, wild fruits, vegetables, vines and medicines. In return for its gifts, the women nurture the forest. They plant taro and yam near the tawn tree because its leaves bring extra nutrients to the soil. Women know which trees in their area give good mulch or other benefits. This familiarity and ancestral "ownership" of the forest gives women the natural right and the know-how to protect land.

II

The claim of rights for particular, generally historically disadvantaged, groups arises out of the factual claim that the members of these groups have special requirements, which the uniform and universal conditions of citizenship in the nation-state are incapable of answering. Hartney (1995) has argued that there are three premises of such claims which must not be conflated: these are the presupposition of the moral importance of groups (recalling the Nozickian critique of utilitarianism for failing to recognize the moral importance of the separateness of persons); the belief that this moral importance generates moral rights and, finally, the issue of whether the protection of groups so defined should take the form of vesting certain legal rights directly in the group or in its members. This last also raises the conceptual issue of the possibility of collective legal rights.

In India we find limited recognition of communities as rights bearing agents.The Constituent Assembly had recognized at least three categories of socially disadvantaged citizens, who by virtue of those disadvantages merit special rights. But, most of these were conceived as negative rights, rather than enabling conditions. This was certainly true of the rights for religious communities to practice and propagate their faith. Members of the Scheduled Castes and Scheduled Tribes, on the other hand, were especially provided for in the form of enabling conditions, though these were couched in paternalist terms, rather than in the vocabulary of rights. The recognition of group claims, defined chiefly in terms of caste/religious community categories, was perforce limited in terms of its potential to generate an agenda of distributive justice. More recently, the enactment of the Muslim (Protection of Divorce) Act, 1986 - in the context of the judgement in the Shah Bano case (1985) - made manifest another dimension of the conflict between individual and group rights, in privileging the rights of cultural community over those of gender equality.

The discourse of rights is fraught with internal tensions due to its genesis in social conflict and the consequently contradictory forms it is obliged to assume in social life. This contradictory character explains both its emancipatory potential and its seemingly limitless capacity to legitimate social inequality and undemocratic economic arrangements. (Bowles and Gintis, 1986).

Today, a distinction is commonly made between three generations of rights. First generation rights, believed to have emerged from the American and French Revolutions, include essentially negative rights, i.e. civil and political rights and liberties. Second generation rights include economic and social rights, and are believed to have emerged from the working-class struggles of the 19th century and the Russian Revolution. The echoes of these are heard in the 'welfare states' of the West in the present century. Third generation rights find partial embodiment in international instruments such as the U.N. Declaration of Rights, or the Algiers Declaration, among many others. These include rights to peace, environment, development, and freedom from hunger. Third generation rights should be read through first-generation rights, and are not expected to be achieved at the expense of the latter.

Rights may justifiably be viewed as part of a 'fraternity of concepts', like freedom, equality, justice, citizenship and democracy. Within the liberal theoretical tradition, as also in liberal political practice, these concepts have been variously emphasized. Resolving the tension between the principles of freedom and equality became important, because the latter often compromised in the name of the former. But should rights necessarily have to suffer similar conceptual fratricide being counterweighed against democracy, rather than being counted together with it?

Rights can have emancipatory potential, depending largely on their location within a larger political project of radical democracy or social justice. Perceptions of the 'failure' of rights to effectuate such a project on its own strength entails not despondency about right themselves, but rather a second look at the social and economic structures that make such an emancipatory politics difficult to achieve. Likewise, the contradictions in the political practice of social movements championing the cause of the displaced, stem as much from their ambiguous social composition as from the confusion regarding the object of rights-claim.

8

The New World of the Migrants

The basic purpose of this study is to explore the socio-economic background of the migrant girls from Chhotanagpur and their aspirations. The focus would be on those girls who start working as domestic workers after getting themselves affiliated to Delhi Domestic Working Women's Forum (DDWWF). The method adopted is through set questionnaires. We interviewed two sets of girls and women —one in the Delhi slums and the other in their villages, when they had gone on holidays after they had already migrated and started working. We asked them about their age and marital status and not only about their own education but also about their husband's and children's. We also wanted to know about their religion, caste and language and whether they are conscious of family planning and their own and their family's health needs. Most important query, of course, was with regard to the causes of migration, their present employment and income and the items on which they spend. Finally, it was necessary to know whether they are happy with the job, with the employer and their life in Delhi - a life so distant and different from what they have left behind

(Please see appendix for the questionnaires). In order to understand the causes of migration, we also tried to find out if their family, or ancestral family, owned any land, forest or trees, and more important. if the land is fertile or rocky. Queries were also about how developed are their villages with regard to their accessibility from the 'developed' outside world.

Socio-Economic Conditions

We talked to 123 women engaged as domestic workers and residing in the slums of Delhi. Oscar Lewis,while writing on culture of poverty,brings out the following features of a slum-

a) provincially and locally oriented

b) marginalised people

c) low literacy

d) less organized

e) people unemployed or under-employed

f) low wages

g) lack of skill

h) no savings,no food reserves

i) attitude of resignation and fatalism,and

j) mistrust of government and acute cynicism.

They belong to the age of 15 years to 50 years, but most of them are in early middle age (30-35 years). Almost all are married and with children. It is a clear indication of the fact that these "housewives" work outside their "household" for the main purpose of supplementing the family income, which is rather low-may be, even below the subsistence level. So much of hard work and the gruelling drudgery of doing the most unproductive work of washing and scrubbing and cooking , both at home and outside, day in and day out, gives them a miserably low return; their monthly cash earning varies from Rs.300 to Rs.650 (only one respondent earned Rs.750). This is a clear proof of the fact that the work of the domestic workers are taken as highly unskilled and unproductive.

This happens mainly due to three reasons or three types of situational problems these hapless women are in - (i) they are economically backward and deprived, (so they have no other option but to accept whatever is offered) (ii) they are illiterate and, above all, (iii) they are women (We are not sure if the fact of they not belonging to the mainstream is of any significance. But in a urban set-up, what matters most is their class and economic identity. After all, power of money and power of exploitation reigns supreme in the "civilized" world. We may, alternately, call it political power).

The three factors, mentioned above, do not allow these women to develop their skills or use their inborn, latent intelligence. They, therefore, are only beggars and can never be choosers. Since they are mostly illiterate and untrained in any vocation they have no option but to go for the most unrewarding and unsatisfying job. They are in this pitiable condition because their parents could not, and nor can they, afford the necessary education and training. More often than not, they do not even have enough to eat or buy medicines. (We all know that, as a result of "developmental" programmes, forests— the natural and free source of their food, fuel and medicines— have either receded or disappeared and the people dependenton forests got displaced.) Besides, (as the study of 133 migrant women in their own villages show), there is hardly any provision for education - not even primary - in the villages. Schools do exist in official records but is there any teacher or teaching? It is an open secret that government schools in the backward areas of India, especially in the tribal areas, are defunct. The road and transport system in these areas are so undeveloped that the tribals cannot even take advantage of the education or health facilities available in the developed areas. People may have to walk as much as 12 to 15 kilometers to reach the main road or to catch a bus, or to reach a post-office - the only possible link with the developed world. Besides, where is the money,motivation or opportunity to take advantage of ,or derive benefit from, the developmental programmes? Yet, two women in our sample are found to have read upto Middle School and ten upto the Primary.

That approximately twelve per cent of this economically backward female population has some degree of education is not a matter to ignore. In all probability, rate of illiteracy would have been hundred per cent if these women were not of tribal origin. The tribals have a great urge for progress, modernity and comfortable living; so they spend much more on education and vocational training than the nontribals. Our study shows that inspite of a very low family income, they try to shelve some money out for the education of their children. Except two, all the children of these mothers are school-going and educated upto a reasonable level. Almost all children (including girls) have read upto primary level; seventeen of the sons and fourteen of the daughters have studied upto middle school and five boys had the opportunity of going for higher education. These figures would have been more encouraging if the tribals in our study were Christians. The Christians have easier access to education because of the widespread activities of the Christian missionaries in these areas for centuries. As a result of exposure to various aspects of life and world through education, they develop an urge and consciousness for education, knowledge and better life.

One conclusion that we can clearly arrive at, by

observing that illiterate mothers (and parents) have literate and reasonably educated children, is that the development programmes, however detrimental for the tribal life-style and livelihood and however opposed the tribals may be towards these, have actually brought a big change in the attitude of these" original inhabitants"; they want to reap maximum benefit out of these (like anybodyelse). They are training themselves to adjust to the demands of the new situation.

Children and their Education

Another encouraging feature of these tribals is that they, unlike most economically and educationally backward people of our country, do not have too many children. The number varies between three and five, though one or two have as many as seven children and a few have only one or two. Gender preference is not obvious the number of sons and daughters is almost equal and there are a few families without a son even! Only 20 percent of them are aware of the scientific family planning methods. Yet the family size, in most cases is limited. This clearly indicates that the tribals have their own indigenous methods of family-planning and that they are culturally conscious of the benefits of a small family. This becomes possible, may be, because of the relatively egalitarian nature of their society; the wife may have a say in the matter of conception. The tribal culture makes both men and women less inhibited about their body and sex. The woman's right over her body, sexuality as well as the right to enjoy are acknowledged. So she is not merely a child-bearing machine.

The pattern of education of their children also points to the same aspect of tribal society, viz: egalitarianism. The tribal parents make no distinction between a son and a daughter with regard to providing them with the opportunity to education, vocation or job. The girls are equally encouraged to leave home for higher education and a job. Rather, our experience with the girls, employed as domestic workers in Delhi, is that semi-educated sisters or daughters migrate to far-off big cities in search of alternative sources of income since very little comes from the small, mostly infertile, land they are left with after becoming victims of the "developmental programmes". The brothers and the men-folk usually stay back to look after land, cattle and trees (if any). We must note at this juncture that the notion of gender equality does not stretch upto the vitals of land and economic rights; women here, like in the non-egalitarian non-tribal societies, are denied any right over land or its produce. So, they are encouraged to leave home in search of income if they have the required motivation, ability & qualifications.

It has already been mentioned that most women (in our sample survey) are married and living with their husbands. Four of them are unmarried, two are widows and one is a divorcee. The divorcee, obviously, is the master of her own household, one widow is independent, the other is under the control of her in-laws and the unmarried are necessarily controlled by the male heads of their families. Interestingly, even some of the married women are in control of, and decision-makers in, their households! This is a typical feature of a tribal society and is invariably absent in the non-tribal, 'Sanskritized societies'. In the latter type, even an earning wife, sister or daughter—even if she is earning more than the male members—has no say in the household expenses nor in any decision-making.

In keeping with the general trend in the societies (tribal or on-tribal) of the under-developed countries, the tribal men of the earlier generations are better off in the field of education. While the majority of the women in our study are illiterates, only 13 men (father or husband) are illiterate. Majority of them have crossed the primary stage, while fifteen have studied upto Middle school.

But, they did not get jobs commensurate with their qualification. Majority are slogging as labourers (sometimes even on their own land as Machiavellian designs of civilization and its agents have systematically robbed them of their own lands). Four out of these are extremely fortunate to get government jobs while three managed to get hold of some loan to set up shops. A few have got employed in factories. We must keep in mind that even this little would not have been possible if not for the Reservation Policy and its partial,thwarted implementation.However sectarian and exploitative our ground-level policies may be, the principles and ideals, solemnly laid down in our Constitution, do act as checks and balances to some extent. Such goals and ideals shine as the Sun of hope and that hope is the most powerful weapon in their endless struggle for what they need and deserve,but are not getting.

It is worth mentioning here that about a fifth of the families own some land in their villages, varying from 6 to 9 acres. A few have some land and cattle and others have only cattle. Needless to say, the number and productive value of the cattle are low. Everybody in our sample belong to the economically deprived strata; so, neither the quality of their land nor the quality of their livestock can be satisfactory. Poverty and low productivity are ever trapped in never-ending vicious circles. The poor do not have money to improve upon their resources and/or work- ability; they do not have adequate income to spend on anything except the bare minimum of food, clothing and shelter and, needless to mention, of the lowest quality.

Displacement - Poverty Causes Migration

The major cause behind steady, large-scale migration of tribal girls/women and even families is poverty or lack of income opportunities in and around their village/dwelling. Almost all of them are lured or brought to Delhi (or, it can be Calcutta) by their relatives, who have already migrated and are working. (It may not be too irrelevant to add here that the tribal migration from Chhotanagpur is seldom to Patna,the capital of Bihar,because they refuse to be considered as part of the political entity called 'Bihar'. They receive as much apathy from their so-called "own" government as they do from the government at the Centre. So they feel most "distant"- both politically and culturally- from their so-called "own" capital, Patna.)

In absolute terms, the new job may not offer them all that better a life, they still may be struggling with want and the absence of so many basic amenities of life. Yet, these migrants feel less burdened with poverty, tension, insecurity and disgracein their new life situation. Psychologically, too, they are better prepared to face these eventualities as it is always more humiliating to be subject of deprivation in one's own hearth and home. They, sort of, taste freedom for the first time as they get the opportunity to interact in a modern urban upper-class cultural milieu (their employers mostly belong to this social stratum).

This section of our society amass wealth and power through questionable means, they are totally devoid of any scruples and get everything in life at the cost of these "have-nots." The have-nots become have-nots and continue to remain have-nots because of the limitless avarice of this privileged section. Yet, this group appears to be liberal, secular and even egalitarian in their day-to-day behaviour if, and so long as, their interests are not at stake. They talk of high ideals, humanitarian causes and even come out on the roads,in their Fab-India clothes, to "fight" for the causes of these have-nots. By their upper-class, consumerist life-style and their deep-rooted sense of private property, they, actually, create the socio-economic conditions against which they feign to mobilize people and put up a crusade.

This is the most pervading pseudo-culture of today So, these tribal women,in their new set-up, enjoy a kind of freedom born out of the disappearance of feudalism.They develop a misleading sense of self-respect, which, they feel, they have lost due to the "dikus", the "development" projects and the consequent loss of their land, forest-products and means of livelihood.

Sense of Freedom

However superficial, futile and misleading this sense of freedom and self-respect may be, it goes deep down into their consciousness and they start finding some kind of roots in their new atmosphere and new home. Most of them are happy, a few are even 'very happy' with their employers. Only five are not happy. The cause may not necessarily be bad treatment by the employer. The more likely cause is that a taste of freedom and comfort creates an urge for more and more and better and better. They start enjoying good clothes, cosmetics, jewellery, movies and other glamorous aspects of urban life. About two-thirds of these workers even their enjoy a sense of security and are happy with life here. This happens due to two reasons (mainly). First,due to the pseudo-cultural compulsions, on the part of their employers,to treat their employees with not too blatant a discrimination (a kind of moral-legal sanction of a democratic society; and secondly, due to the strict terms and conditions insisted upon by DDWWF. As a sharp contrast, there is nobody,back home,to protect them from the atrocities of the dikus and the onslaughts of the "Nation's development." Only fifty per cent of these women would like to return to their home and hearth even if they are re-offered a means of earning there.They ask who or what is going to chalk out and enforce working conditions in their favour and who or what is going to protect them from possible discrimination and exploitation ? Work on land, at construction sites or in the factories (the sort of work they usually get) call for much strenuous physical labour and much longer hours of work. As domestic workers, they get reasonably good food and comfortable living conditions, also.

It is necessary to mention here that though the main cause behind migration is poverty or absence of a means of livelihood at home, a few migrate due to some family problems-may be discord with the male head of the family (father, brother or husband) or any other close relative. A sense of self-respect and an urge for freedom, i.e. consciousness as an individual, are implied in this. As a contrast, most women of the non-tribal society quietly and non-challantly put up with this kind of family or patriarchal dominance/oppression. We do not mean to suggest that the tribal women are rebellious like the women's libbers; but they, definitely, prefer venturing out to a new world and an independent life-situation if they get an opportunity.

Interestingly, most of the families (about two-thirds) do not stop their women from migrating. They know, from the experiences of those who have migrated earlier, that their girls can provide some cushioning to the terribly fragile economic condition of the family. As mentioned earlier, the families, unless they are migrating en bloc, prefer their daughters, rather than their sons, to move out of home in search of an extra income. First, the men-folk prefer to work on the little land that may still be in the possession of the family; after all ploughing cannot be done by the women (the tribals of this region follow customs and beliefs very much similar to those of the Hindus). Secondly men, usually, are not preferred as domestic workers. When they migrate they normally end up working as labour in the construction sites - the physical labour is as hard (may be even harder) as it is while working on land for agricultural production. The working and living conditions are no better and the money earned is too little to give them any incentive to leave their home and land. (The domestic workers, on the contrary, are in a position to save their entire income or to send it home). There is not even the compensatory factor of feeling "at home" (in the literal sense of the term). They do not even enjoy the psychological comfort of harping on community support even amidst the dikus. Above everything else, what the tribals - both men and women - cannot digest is the dehumanizing terms and conditions of work and the consequent loss of all self-respect or identity. Such a situation is analogous to landing from frying pan to fire.

The relatively comfortable and non-oppressive working and living conditions of the domestic workers, thus, make both the girls and their families happy. These working girls are treated with extra affection and as an honoured guest, when they visit their families and villages. It is like a special event in their families' life that their daughter/sister lives in a big city, has become "urbane and sophisticated", wears "fashionable" clothes, jewellery and make-up and is earning enough money to spend on herself and also to send home. She looks so different and even talks so differently and herself feels proud of being so different. In most cases, the girls prefer going back to their employment in the city and not stay back in their villages.

A very small proportion, face an indifferent family attitude i.e. their families do not care much for the transformations that have taken place in these girls. These families are not unhappy about it, either. The struggle for livelihood is so hard for them that a change in the lifestyle or attitude of the earning females of their families does not make things different for them. The little extra money that is sent to them cuts little dent into their poverty and deprivation.

Two families are unhappy about the migration of their daughters. They are so deeply conscious and proud of their tribal identity that they find little reason to understand or appreciate the change that the upper-class urban atmosphere brought in the female migrants of their family. The intensity of their poverty, deprivation and resultant desperation is so acute that the money sent to them is able to bring little change in their day-to-day living conditions. Their consumption needs are so high, the amount of loans accumulated is so voluminous that any flow of money and/ or consumer items is never enough. Their empty life-situation has made them empty of any emotions or sentiments.Since the society only takes away from them without giving them anything in return,they lose the sense of reciprocity. They do not treat these girls well, nor do these girls have much eagerness or attachment left for their village or their earlier pattern of life.

Self-Confidence and Ambition

The confidence that these domestic workers develop, due to their freedom with money and exposure to urban, upper-class attitude and morality, fills them with ambition. They are, all the time, looking for a better job, more money and, therefore, a better life of comfort and consumerism. More than two-thirds of these girls are constantly looking for a change of job. These domestic workers change employers every now and then, on the slightest pretext. They keep pressurizing the employers for greater and greater monetary and other benefits. In most cases they succeed. First,(as already mentioned) the employers belong to the pseudo-culture of socialistic behaviour or in other words, a kind of a humane treatment of the hapless, (though with a condescending attitude). Secondly, they belong to that category of social class where domestic work is considered drudgery and below dignity (even if it is at one's own home);so they got to employ somebody at any cost. And, therefore, thirdly,a few hundreds extra demanded by the worker is nothing really for them as their monthly earnings run into thousands, if not lakhs.

The negative aspect of this kind of market behaviour is that these migrants, mostly, do not have the ambition of improving their skills or educational qualifications; they do not realize that they can change over to a more meaningful and respectable job/career if they invest on making themselves more capable instead of wasting their income on consumer and inessential items only. These girls even tend to forget that they had migrated to such a far-off and unfriendly place in order to help their families to survive or, may be, to invest, for better production, on their land. This,unfortunately, is bound to happen as a sense of freedom, born out of economic independence and gender-consciousness, knows no bounds. The trait is more pronounced in women, as economic domination by men over women is the very foundation of patriarchy; women, her body and soul—all are regarded as man's property. The 'newly free' girls do not foresee or realize that this kind of freedom becomes fragile and short-lived unless the skills for acquiring and retaining this freedom are developed. The commitment to freedom and against all kinds of exploitation has to be deep and firm.

The basic philosophy on which community action for development is based is that the poor and the powerless are:

a) capable of taking action and bringing change

b) capable of rising above social,religious and political prejudices to fight for a common cause

c) capable of throwing up a local leadership

d) capable of consciously designing programmes to eradicate apathy and lack of motivation

e) capable of breaking petty individualistic walls to achieve a certain degree of freedom and power.

(Devasia—"Empowering women for sustainable development")

Although majority of the migrants who are registered with DDWWF (Delhi Domestic Working Women's Forum) profess Christianity (having been educated, modernized, employed and to a certain extent, empowered by the Catholic Churches working for centuries with the oppressed in the tribal and backward areas), we had chosen a group of Hindus in our first sample. We cannot really brand them as Hindus, as they actually profess their own religious and social customs and beliefs. It is a well-known census trick that dialects, similar to Hindi, are clubbed as Hindi, and religious rituals, similar to those of the Hindus, are dubbed as Hindu. The policy-makers and decision-takers in our political system overwhelmingly belong to the "Hindi-Hindu" belt and syndrome. Communities, geographically belonging to this region, are expected to bow down or subscribe to the "mainstream culture." The most effective, but apparently non-violent, way to erasing the tribal, low caste or minority identity is by getting them amalgamated in the dominant milieu. The greater is this attempt the stronger is the resistance on the part of these marginalised groups, though a few, who managed to climb up the ladder of educational excellence and economic prosperity, copy and imbibe the values and life-styles of the urbane, upper-class non tribals.

Our study tells us that social interaction (i.e. friendship and help to each other) of the is usually with the migrants from the neighbouring Hindi-speaking States like Haryana, Rajasthan, Uttar Pradesh. the largest number in this group, needless to mention, is from the tribal regions of South Bihar. Marriages mostly are within the communities and in most cases, the necessary rituals and ceremonies take place back in the villages.

One encouraging feature about this group is that education (whatever may be its level) has not fallen flat on them. These women, inspite of their awfully unhygienic living conditions (in the slums,) are reasonably conscious of health and hygiene. About fifty per cent of them regularly go for periodic medical check-ups and treatments whenever necessary. (The DDWWF arranges for such facilities to its registered members). The disheartening feature about these women is that they are not fully aware or keen about family planning and its methods. Only a fifth in our sample seem to be. It is strange that such educated and health-conscious women—are so little conscious of the fact that greater the number of children/dependents in a family less are the quantity and the quality of food and other things needed for living. Is it because these migrants, though landless, have not got rid of the the typical 'farmer' belief that more mouths to feed means more hands to work on land? They do not have to pay to the labour, as family labour is always free? And, that is how, they are actually earning more?

We know such belief or notion is based on naive understanding of the hard realities. They are simple, innocent, illiterate or semi-educated people, untrained in the logic of economics. Even if they are educated to a certain level, they being rural do not have the mental make-up or training to people understand the right kind of economics.

A rather encouraging fact about this group is the parents (in our sample) are not in favour of child-labour; they usually send their children to schools or non-formal education centres even if they are pressed under hard economic conditions. Why then the women in our study, are, in general, not bothered about family planning? Can we deduce that it is a subconscious protest against the onslaught from the mainstream? If they have been forced to lose their home and hearth, they do not want to lose in terms of number? The tribal population should not dwindle? Even if they lose out to the "development" projects of the "civilized" world, they should not look too inconsequential in their numerical strength; their protests must appear to be a force — both in terms of number and the strength of unity—to reckon with? This appears to be a plausible reason. (It is not irrelevant to mention here that all minorities, facing the cultural and other onslaughts from the majority community, suffer from this uncomfortable psychology. The reasons behind are not really unreasonable).

9

The New World For the Migrants

In our earlier Chapter we attempted to delve into the causes behind migration, and the migrants' pattern of living and level of satisfaction/dissatisfaction after migration. We also tried to bring to the readers' knowledge, how and to what extent, these girls, working as domestic workers, get affected by the upper class living and thinking of their employers.

In this section we shall try to understand the mentality of similar such migrant women in the background of their own home and culture. We have interviewed about 130 women (ranging between the ages of 13 to 67 years, but mostly middle-aged) from Gumla, Ranchi and Jamtara/Dumka. We had taken a few village/area specific indicators and tried to assess the mentality and attitude of these women in the context of excessive economic backwardness of the places where they were born and brought up. It is definitely interesting and worthwhile to study these women when their thinking about life is not yet over-shadowed by the lure of the glamour of upper-class city-life. It makes a completely different study when they are back in their own familiar background. They can re-assess their worth and their ambitions in the context of the harsh reality of their true life situation. A comparative study of these two types of migrant groups viz: from a few slums of Delhi and a few areas in Chhotanagpur, gives us a more or less comprehensive picture of the problem.

Two-thirds of these working women interviewed belong to the dominant tribal group, viz. the Mundas. There are 37 Oraons (known to be most upwardly mobile in the field of education) and only 12 Kharias and 5 Santhals in our sample. Historically and also at present, the Mundas are most active in politics and protest movements. Protest is a consciousness, or even a realization, of one's

a) rights

b) denial of rights

c) the need to get oneself armed with rights so that one can retain or regain one's identity.

This consciousness, when shared and/or organized,can arm people with the power of confidence and show them the right method and strategy. Such protest movements can not only liberate but can also bring about some needed social reformations. The strong walls of patriarchy, supported by the firm beams of capitalism and imperialism, got to be shattered if liberation has to be lasting and meaningful. Birsa Munda has become a legend and a symbol. He is synonymous to any kind of tribal anger, unrest and movement.

The choice of so many Mundas in our study is purely accidental; but it is not untrue that Mundas, in general, are more educated, confident and fearless and that the majority of the women/girls leaving their homes and villages in search of a less oppressive life are Mundas only. In keeping with the tradition of Birsa Munda, the Mundas, closely followed by the Oraons, are much more intolerant of the demands of "outside" civilization.

The next significant point to note (while studying this second set of samples) is that 123 out of the 130 are Christians, the rest holding on to their indigenous religion called "Sarna". It should not become difficult for our readers to understand why this feature is specially worth noting because we have already discussed, at quite a length, how the Christians (the Catholics) among the tribals are at an advantageous position in the realms of health care and education. The side-effects of proselytization were extremely beneficial for these forest-dwellers, as neither the governments nor the mainstream ever cared to do anything worth the name for them.

Our survey showed that most of the tribal villages, with the exception of one or two, did not have a school beyond the primary level, and in most cases, only the four walls and a roof of the so-called school building existed; there was neither a blackboard nor furniture. On paper, teachers are appointed (though most of the schools have only one teacher and a helper), but they hardly ever report to their duties. Even if some of them come, as a routine, to the school-building, they are not able to motivate the students. They, themselves, are not motivated enough. So, students are mostly absent and the drop-out rate is alarmingly high. This becomes a further demotivating factor both for the teachers and the students. They find the system and the accompanying operation highly farcical. The children feel it is better to play than to waste time and energy for travelling up and down to a non-functioning school; the poverty-stricken parents feel it is better if their children work and earn some money during the time they "waste" in school.

The Christian tribals do not usually suffer from this disadvantage; they enjoy the privilege of special care and attention from the Christian missionaries, who are usually very much committed to the cause of health and education to the marginalised of our society. But poverty, ignorance and superstitions create such a backward pull that only a little over fifty percent are literate or educated. Most, in our sample, have got primary education, forty have studied upto Middle School and only eleven up to High School; A few have been motivated enough to go for vocational training. A few tribal villages in the Bhagalpur district have specifically expressed their deep gratitude to the Christian missionaries for the education, vocational training and motivational push they received and thus benefited. They are particularly grateful because these "benefactors" do not hesitate to penetrate into the remote interior areas where no other social-worker or government emissary enters.

The inhabitants of these backward areas have to walk 12 to 15 kilometers (sometimes even 20 kilometers) to reach the nearest place of modern civilization, viz. post office, market or main road from where one can board a bus or a train. This is an important reason why most of these women do not intend to go back to their villages once they get a taste of the comfort and convenience of town or city life.

There is no doubt that poverty and loss or lack of earning opportunities is the main cause behind migration, but one cannot, and should not, ignore the fact that education and vocational training create the right kind of confidence and motivation to do a job according to one's capability and inclination - thus breaking the age-old pattern of livelihood and thinking. Different kinds of jobs and different kinds of surroundings cause changes in life-styles. The sense of independence, born out of earning and living independently — away from the bindings of their own community — slowly and gradually effect a change in their beliefs, thinking and attitude to life. For better or for worse, they get slowly amalgamated to the overwhelming mainstream culture; but not without a sense of shock and protest every now and then. They are not able to quarantine themselves from the very influences that rob them of their culture and identity; at the same time, they are not even able to surrender totally. In fact, harder the onslaught, stronger become their sense of identity and the preparedness to protest.

The Christian tribals are not only better-off in their educational status than their non-Christian sisters, they are also better-off financially. Almost all of them own land, varying between 1 to 5 acres. The quality of land in that generally rugged area is not all that bad. As many as thirty six of them own fertile, productive land and twenty nine have access to lands of mixed quality. Twelve reaped reasonable amount of benefit from the cluster of trees (timber or medicinal or both) they continued to own in addition to the land they cultivated. Here also education and the confidence that education gave them, made them better-equipped to stand up against exploitation and deprivation. Education and the associated confidence made them conscious and knowledgeable about their rights not merely as original inhabitants (adivasis) but also as citizens of a democratic country where special rights and benefits are guaranteed to them in its Constitution.

Unlike the women in our previous sample (viz. those residing in the Delhi slums), the women under our present discussion are better equipped - both mentally and financially - to spend on things other than the bare necessities of food and shelter. Quite a good number of them also spend wisely on health and education. About a third of them even have the good sense of investing on land and farming. A very small number waste their meagre income on "destructive" things like loan - repayment and social customs and rituals. This not only shows that their economic condition is not all that unmanageable, but also that education has given them the right kind of enlightenment from superstitious and socio-religious obscurantism. Education, if it generates modern and secular thought process and attitude, better income and greater confidence, leads to still better income, better education, a higher degree of awareness and still greater sense of self-respect and confidence. This process has the potential of going on and on and spiraling upwards and upwards. Human potential and the momentum towards progress know no bounds. We can, perhaps, call this trend a "virtuous cycle" But, unfortunately, it hovers in the range of possibilities and remains an ideal or a Utopia. The forces of capitalism and patriarchy are so powerful that, in reality, the poor always gets poorer and the rich always get richer; the privileged and the powerful have the privilege and the power to see to it that their power and privilege go on increasing. So the deprived continue to get more deprived. Vicious or virtuous, the cycle always gets trapped in its own circle.

A powerful force of consciousness, born out of education, experience and the self-confidence which, in turn gets generated because of the first two, can sometimes break this circle. The fact that the tribal society is less divisive and less oppressive and, therefore, they are somewhat armed with courage and confidence to fight the situation better cannot be ignored in this context.

In our sample, a little less than half the families spend on food and the unavoidable necessities only, about half spend also on health and related things, and thirty spend on the education of their children apart from food, clothes, shelter and health. And as many as nineteen families - not a very insignificant number considering their generally backward economic condition - have the wisdom to invest their little mite for the betterment of the quality of their land. If education and training could be widespread and meaningful and if they could get opportunity to earn according to their qualifications, motivation and endeavour, how 'virtuous' all the 'vicious' circles would have turned into, and we would have seen 'people's' empowerment and 'peoples'' government in the real sense of the term.

Unlike in the earlier sample, their situation vis-a-vis their families at home is not very congenial. About seven families are positively hostile to their girls who have migrated and are living on their own. The reasons are not clearly known. The most likely reason is the families' disapproval of the change in their attitudes and lifestyles (which is because of their interaction with the non-tribal upper class urban culture.)

We have already discussed that these migrants, who work as domestic workers, develop a tendency to get themselves moulded in the culture of their employers or in the culture of their surrounding. It may be a subconscious process through which these tribals are imbibing the values which are alien to theirs. They get alienated from their own people, but they do not want to remain alienated from the mainstream. The purpose and the process of alienation, in this manner, complete a full circle. Since the non-migrants have not tasted the freedom employment, even in the "alien" society, can give - the freedom due to the easy earning (however little) as well as due to the interaction with the upper-class urban society— they cannot, naturally, understand why the migrants from their society have chosen the path of a change in their life-style and attitudes.

The tribals are found to be rather proud, possessive and conservative of their own culture and tradition. But they are equally keen for a modern and better life if opportunities come in their way. They are fond of all the good things in life, they have an inborn knack about how to enjoy life and they are always looking for opportunities to enjoy life. They are fond of good food, fashionable clothes and all other comforts and enjoyment that modern urban living can provide. So, a much greater number of families (three times more) are happy with those who have migrated and are earning.

They are happy even if some of these girls do not send money to their families at home. The family just likes the idea of a member being different and distinct, earning and independent, urbanized and modernized. They treat their migrated girls, when they return home or come for a visit, as guests of honour; they feel proud of the "capabilities" of their daughters/sisters. They proudly show to their friends, neighbours and relatives the gifts (fashionable clothes, cosmetics, steel utensils, crockery and cutlery and a few electronic gadgets, even) that their daughters/sisters bring from the cities out of their *own* earning on which no man,no patriarch,no custom or tradition has any say. This is a great leap forward in the path of women's emancipation.

There is no doubt that the girls migrate with the sole purpose of helping the family,which is always in dire need of something or other. There is a moral binding though, there is no social obligation. Since the girls are at a physical distance from their family, community or society, they can never be forced to send or spend their income for their family or for anybodyelse. We know, too well, how women even in the highly educated middle-class families, living in an externally obvious atmosphere of freedom,do not, generally, have a right over their hard-earned income; it is merged in the family income pool and they have no right to decide how much will be spent on which heading. It is really "hard-earned" as they are not freed from their kitchen and other domestic duties inspite of working outside. Even if their opinions are taken, they, invariably, have a secondary role to play. This is a factor of no mean significance. It is not too uncommon that quite a good number of girls do not really look forward to going back to their familiar surrounding, as they would not like to be tied down by any uncomfortable obligation. Not only that they would not like to give up their newly acquired life-style, they also would not like to marry the rural,backward boys and get tied down to the tradition.

They, thus, prefer marrying a boy who has also weaned himself away from the "backward pulls" of his society. They find themselves special and distinct, and enjoy the envy and jealousy in the eyes of the other tribals in the village.

Unfortunately the urbanised 'adivasis' fail to realize that this semi-voluntary integration with the mainstream ethos and culture which, undoubtedly, is the unwelcome effect of the "development" process and globalization, is detrimental to their very identity and existence. But we need to look at it from another angle also. The copying and imbibing of the mainstream culture and thought process can possibly offer them an opportunity to reap the benefits of "development " and "modernization." The tribals migrate with that hope, they try to adapt themselves to the upper-class urban culture with that hope. But once deprived, they are always deprived. The logic of capitalism, economic imperialism and globalization is that the "have"s have more and more and the "have-nots" have less and less. The "have"s build a strong fortress around them so that there can be no new entrant to their privileges. They will tighten their security the moment they fear or foresee a new entrant. In fact, their tireless endeavour will be to flush out as many as they can. The important corollary to the logic of capitalism and imperialism is that there will be a concentration of wealth and power in the hands of fewer and fewer .

These migrant girls, when they go back home - mostly on a holiday or due to some emergency in the family - talk a lot and in details about the "comfortable' living at their employers' and about the "fun" of freedom and city-life. They talk of the sundry movies that they see—both on the big and the small screens — of the restaurants, amusement parks and other glamours of a city-life and the freedom they enjoy in making friends and even having boy-friends. They also show the showy saris and cosmetic jewellery that they can afford to buy because of their "own" income. Above all, they make it very clear to their friends and cousins that they enjoy a "special" treatment at home because of their earning and contribution to the family-income. This "special" position is also because of the sense of pride that most of their family-members have because of a daughter/sister who is so different from those who have not migrated and also quite similar - or, rather, nearer - to those who enjoy position of power and influence in the society which control their life and destiny. They find this phenomenon rather unwelcome and unfortunate, but they also know that this is their fate; they are fully aware of their helplessness in this situation. Their life-situation has taught them that they are trapped in the labyrinth of the mainstream development process. They have slid down to the nadir of deprivation and once deprived they will always remain deprived - the extent and the intensity of this will go on increasing as development in the capitalist framework continues to spread its tentacles. A dying man catches at a straw. So, these tribals hold on to whatever little they manage to get from the otherwise hostile system.

A majority of these girls get lured to the glamour of city-life as well as to the prospect of bringing some money to the family which is surviving below the subsistence level. Their friends, who are already working as domestic workers, serve as the chief motivators. They are also introduced to the Delhi Domestic Working Women's Forum (DDWWF) by their friends. Some of them are called by their relatives or family-members. They may be offering their labour at the construction sites or working as part-time domestic help. A few are inspired by the Christian missionaries who have been responsible for the education of these girls before they migrated. They may be taken care of by such bodies, if further vocational training is required. There are quite a few Christian charitable organizations which offer scholarships for computer and other vocational trainings or provide free boarding and lodging to the girls who intend to train themselves up for an useful income. This kind of education, training and motivation help these girls to build up a sense of confidence and an urge to do better in life. The tribal girls, interviewed at Bhagalpur (Bihar) have expressed their deep gratitude to these missionaries for putting some meaning in their otherwise empty lives.

10

Work and the Status of Women

"Work" can be defined as "the active, labour-based interaction of human beings with the material world" (Geeta Menon). Hence, the history of human work participation is the history of interactions of human-beings with nature and various production-oriented human organizations. Work, in its earliest context, was limited to food procurement and protection of human lives. Even now, in its broadest and all-pervasive sense, work refers to human activities for the purposes of survival, living and security. It can also include entertainment, pleasure and pursuit of finer human sensibilities.

Among the hunting-gathering tribes, the sources of food were the forest-products (like abundant variety of fruits, nuts, wild-flowers, leaves, roots and tubers, mushrooms) and wild animals (like rodents, reptiles, birds). Most of these (both tree products and animals) served as medicines also. The items/headings or the broader details of work (more or less for every human being) have changed, but the categories of work, whether for the ancient man or for the modern man, have remained the same...over so many centuries ! They are

(1) food procurement

(2) protection of life, property and territory.

(3) child-bearing and rearing, which includes the maintenance of basic health standards

(4) the activities of food-processing and distribution, house-construction, fencing, care of livestock, maintenance of sanitation and physical cleanliness, etc. are taken as "extension" activities of the first three main activities.

According to feminist contention "man-the-hunter" was projected as the main bread-winner at the cost of "woman-the-gatherer". Women, thus, was projected as the passive recipient of the productive activities of men. But, according to the feminist counter-argument, it was actually "woman - the - gatherer" who was the source of *sustained* food -supply. Women, who gathered fruits, nuts, edible leaves, flowers, mushrooms, roots, tubers, etc., could be depended upon to provide daily sustenance, while meat was merely a supplementary food-item, depending on providence and availability. Only 20 to 40 per cent of calories consumed by the hunting-gathering communities come from meat or animal-product (Geeta Menon). Besides, the early food-production (agricultural) techniques (prevalent even now among a few tribal communities in the North-East) used to be "slash-and burn" and that was primarily women's responsibility or a "female farming" system. Women, in fact, used to combine food-gathering or the collection of forest-produce with "slash and burn" agriculture.

The plough is characteristic only of the European and dominant Asiatic civilizations, in opposition to "bewar" (slash-and-burn cultivation). We can brand settled agriculture as one of the main introducers of "inequality", because it brings in "private ownership" and the concept of "property". Property, by its very nature, is the most obvious and most powerful source of "power". The other source is physical strength. Because of physical strength, men started grabbing and accumulating things, which came to be known as property ever since the label of private ownership got attached to those. As an inevitable consequence came socio-cultural restrictions on women's economic participation. The actual quantity/burden of their work did not go down - rather it went up with increasing male-domination over women - but their contribution got devalued. Socio-religious sanctions were put against women's work and men's work were eulogized, so that women remain eternally subservient to men.

Women were debarred from ploughing and sowing. Similarities were drawn with human reproductive system. Ploughing and sowing were like insemination, though the field (earth), which was compared to the womb, was the main producer. Tedious and tiring jobs like weeding and transplanting, collecting firewood and water, cooking washing and rearing of children were considered female jobs and therefore, of low status and prohibited to men. No production value, that is why, is attached to this kind of work. Is any "productive" i.e. with value-tag attached to it, job possible without the support of the "unproductive" (female) works - however invisible and unrecognized these may be?

Division of labour and private ownership of land and other properties were significant bench-marks in the path of patriarchy, which is regarded as 2,500 years long. Division of labour established surely and firmly the notion of gender, in other words, the unbridgeable division between man and woman created by the mere coincidence of being born as such; the full development of private property established the full control of man over woman. The State and its machinery endorsed this status with all the political and economic powers in its hands. Gerda Lerner, in her book "The Creation of Patriarchy" (1986) says, "the first appropriation of private property consists of the appropriation of the labour of women as *reproducers*." The subordination of women long preceded the formation of class-society and class oppression. Women are the first historic category of *non-owning* workers. According to Manu, the wife and the slave are unpropertied - whatever they earn is the property of those to whom they belong. The particular tribal society in our study is, surprisingly though, no exception to this.

Male ownership of women's property and of women as property, extends to the body and life of women, specially to her fertility and sexuality; and this is the birth place of male-violence. Violence and torture are the most effective ways of keeping anybody under control. The custom of 'women only' be branded as witches came as a rather effective method of depriving women - particularly the single, deserted or widowed - from any possible share in the property. Such women are declared insane and sent to lunatic asylums even by some of the educated, middle-class families.

The tribal communities (in this area) are breaking up due to their alienation from the land and forests. If women , *too*, are given land, it will check this dangerous process. Thus, a positive, collective and rational path of national development can be paved.

The effect of settled agriculture and private ownership of property on women's body, mind and socio-economic status got many times accentuated as a result of the commercialization of the forest resources (started during the colonization of India by the British and continued to this day due to the 'pro-propertied- class' policies of our "own" governments - at the Centre and in the State). Do we really own our government and can the governments claim to own its people? The common people and their wishes and aspirations are supposed to be the very foundation of democracy. How far democratic is our democracy? Will it remain a utopia for ever? The "culture" of profit-maximization and accumulation of wealth marks a complete imbalance in "cultural ecology", thus throwing the tribal communities - which believe in community ownership and egalitarian share in the benefits - into a process of all-pervasive and extensive changes. This is devastating for the tribal economy and culture; in the long run, it is devastating for the national economy and national ethos also. A policy that turns a substantial section of the population into "have-nots", cannot but be devastating for the overwhelming majority who are already "have-nots."

Women are have-nots even among the have-nots, because historically and traditionally women are denied the vital rights of taking decisions and a share in her family income. Women, in whichever economic class, are, thus, completely dependent on men, resulting in their lack of bargaining power even in matters of marriage, divorce and remarriage, etc. not to speak of the absence of any rights,whatsoever, in matters related to land,other properties and her personal or family income. Deserted women are doomed to become economic destitutes since they can claim rights to neither natal nor conjugal property. (Women in some of the tribes did have rights before the onslaught of capitalism-imperialism)

Women's work can be looked at in several ways: one is to look at the different economic sectors in which most of the poor women work; another is to understand the nature of labour and production relations under which women work; yet another way could be to classify women's work on the basis of the location of work itself.

(1) Agriculture is the major economic sector for

millions (20 m. in 1981) of poor rural women, who perform all tedious and back-breaking jobs, except ploughing, which is a male privilege.

The division of labour is accompanied by a number of taboos for women. The asymmetric nature of the taboos, for there are no corresponding taboos for men, shows that they are meant to establish an unequal ordering, a definite hierarchy in the family. The prohibition on ploughing is universal. Among the Ho and Munda a woman must not even touch the plough. Mere accidental touching of the plough can be a serious matter to be taken up by the village panchayat; so as to minimize the chances of accidentally touching the plough, it is kept outside the house. Sachhidanand mentions an incident when a man, in the absence of his wife, took his crying baby girl on his hip while he was ploughing. "For this (indirect) female 'touch' of the plough he was taken to task." (1979) Among the Santhal, Oraon and Kharia there is no taboo against women touching the plough. They can and often do carry the plough (on their heads though not on their shoulders) to the field. But they must not touch a yoked plough. Santhal, and other tribal women cannot thatch a roof or use a leveller. "They may not shoot arrows, use a razor, chisel holes, strike an axe or fish with line and hook. They cannot weave cloth or string a cot."

(Gender and Tribe)

(2) Many more, about 75 million (1981) women, are engaged in dairy farming, and about 15 million in animal husbandry i.e. taking care of domestically productive animals like goats, sheep, hens, etc.

(3) Forestry or the collection of forest products, as we know, is a female domain; tribal women are particularly involved in it - even emotionally. Planting new trees and taking care of the existing

ones is their passion (as is apparent in the famous "Chipko" movement).

(4) About 8 lakhs women are engaged in the cultivation and rearing of silk cocoons and related operations. It is a growing sector. About 20 lakhs are engaged in khadi and village enterprises like spinning, bee-keeping, mat-making, etc. Weaving, but, is a male domain. Women are the backbone to the handloom industry though actual weaving is not allowed to them. Quite a few social service arganisations give training in weaving to women only, with the dual purpose of breaking this takoo and income-generation for this economically deprived sex.

(5) A variety of traditional handicraft activities like embroidery, lace-making, block-printing, grass, bamboo and cane-products are performed by rural and urban women.

(6) While the "macho" activity of fishing on the sea is done by men (they appear brave and heroic like in the case of hunting in olden days) the non-glamorous works like net-making, fish-drying and vending are done mostly by women.

Among the Mundas there is no prohibition against women touching weapons or using them - though they must not step over them. But all the other tribes have prohibitions on women handling some or all weapons. Among the Santhal, the crucial bow and arrow is prohibited to women. It is only on the occasion of the ritual, *jani shikar* (women's hunt) which takes place once in twelve years that women are allowed to handle the weapons. (Gender and Tribe)

(7) The most prescribed sector for women is the urban informal and unorganized because wages are low, service-conditions are deplorable and the work is not evaluated in GNP.

(a) A large number of poor women - particularly agricultural and construction labour, work at no fixed rate which is, invariably, much lower than what men get for the same work.

Another reason for their low earning is that they are paid on "piece-rate" basis, while men are paid on "time rate" basis. When a skill is identified with women it ends up in being valued less.

A third reason is that women are made to believe that (i) their work is unimportant or secondary to the nation's productive process, (ii) that the work is a past-time while gossiping and that their earnings are poor supplements to the family income (though, in reality, most of the urban poor households survive on the woman's income, as men squander their income (which in money terms, is much more) in drinking, gambling and sundry other vices or non-essential expenditure.

(b) Women of this economic stratum work along an "invisible assembly line" where she is assigned to make only a small component part of the whole product. They are linked to traders through agents who supply raw materials, collect finished products and pay wages at piece-work rate. Women are thus duped to remain deprived of the opportunities to develop their overall skill or to be part of the nation's production process. Garment- making, bidi-rolling and collecting minor forest produce are a few examples of the type of unproductive assignments women are usually engaged in.

Structural adjustment policies or the New Economic policy of our government has affected women's employment and socio-economic position adversely. Wages for women have gone down further as rise in prices and deregulation of the labour market are forcing women to accept whatever little they can earn; after all, they have no option but to take care of their family, though, according to all religious sanctions and social expectations, the responsibility of the family is male privilege and prerogative. Women are subjugated precisely because of this responsibility which men must undertake..... To add to the misery of the poor and the women, social subsidies like fair-price shops, are getting discontinued, the public sector-units are getting closed and home and cottage industries are getting discouraged; the preferences of those with buying power are increasingly for the glamorous products of the latest technologies,and not for aesthetics.

(c) In case of family-labour women's work remain totally unrecognized and, therefore, invisible.

Table 1: **Average Labour* days spent by women and men**

Type of Work	**Women**	**Men**
Shifting cultivation	213.57	96.88
Wage Labour	52.14	106.92
Firewood collection	135.12	61.57
Other forest produce	108.09	90.09
Others	11.33	63.09

Source: Fernandes and Menon, 1987.

* These are not humandays because they spend four to six hours a day on these activities for the average number of days given here.

(Gender and Tribe)

(d) Overwhelming majority of poar women are self-employed (60%). Regular employees constitute only 4%, while casual labourers account for 30%. That is how they remain unorganized, unskilled and, therefore, most exploited.

Their income is at the subsistence level since they get no value for their labour, enterprise or skill. There is hardly any scope for skill-development since they remain unguided. Field experiences of NGOs and social workers suggest that women's economic security or freedom cannot be ensured or enhanced by projects that focus merely on income. Empowerment is absolutely necessary. Easy access to credit and services like creches have to go hand in hand with awareness raising, organization-building and unionization. It is important to see employment and empowerment as mutually supportive for the purposes of promoting a woman's life-situation.

Gender division of labour makes "domestic work" an exclusive female domain, even among the Mundas, Hos, Oraons and Kharias of the Jharkhand region - not just among the caste Hindus. Men, *as a rule* do not participate in the domestic labour of cleaning, cooking and child care. They may do these only if their women are unwell or unable to do due to some compulsive reason. Santhals are a bit progressive. Men, off and on, help women in household chores like fetching water or pounding rice; as a rule, they look after children when the women are cooking. The women, even married daughters, seem to be having the right to income, or the benefit form her labour. Income from forest produce accrues entirely to the person who collects and sells. There is no restriction on women taking grain from the "mara" or the family-granary. With the other communities, father or brother *may* keep some land/property for a woman, for the eventuality of her marriage breaking down. But the woman cannot claim it as a matter of right. The woman can have some claim to land/property in case of she being deformed or disabled.

The obstacles that the economically deprived and the socially backward classes (which, in general include the SCs, STs and the women) face while struggling for upliftment and empowerment are (in a nutshell)

01) Undeveloped traditional skills and absence of new skills

02) Little or no access to technical skill or technical extension services

03) Lack of adequate and appropriate tools or work-place

04) Lack of management skills or lack of confidence

05) Lack of access to production inputs

06) No ownership or control of means of production

07) Inavailability of raw-materials and their high cost

08) Lack of storage facilities

09) No access to credit due to the ignorance about the institutional sources of finance and the diffidence about how to go about it

10) Unplanned and unguided utilization of loans if, of course, they manage to get

11) Absence of the knowledge about market

12) Exploitative market behaviour (dominated by men)

13) Access only to the unorganized labour market

14) Low, gender-unfriendly wages and inadequate employment opportunities

15) Inadequate and gender-insensitive support services like absence of, or poor quality of, day-care, legal-aid and health-care services

16) And, above all, stiff, cut-throat competition from the industrial and private sectors.

The "Human Development Report" of 1995, brought out by the United Nations, endorses the views elaborated above. It says

* Poverty has a woman's face - of 1.3 billion people in poverty, 70% are women. The increasing poverty

among women has been linked to their unequal situation in the labour market, the treatment they get under social welfare systems and their status and power in the family.

* Women's labour force participation has risen by only four percentage points in 20 years - from 36% in 1970 to 40% in 1990. Compare that with a two-thirds increase in female adult literacy and school enrollment.
* Women receive a disproportionately small share of credit from formal banking institutions. They are assumed to have no collateral to offer- despite working much harder than men. For example, in Latin America and the Caribbean islands, women constitute only 7-11% of the beneficiaries of credit programmes.
* Women normally receive a much lower average wage than men, because they hold low-paying jobs or work in the informal sector; they are usually paid less than men for equal work. The average female wage is only three-fourths of the male wage in the non-agricultural sector in 55 countries that have comparable data.
* All regions record a higher rate of unemployment among women than men.
* In developing countries women constitute less than a seventh of the administrators and managers.
* Women occupy only 10% of the parliamentary seats and only 6% of the cabinet positions.
* In 55 countries, there are either no woman in parliament or fewer than 5%. These countries range from very poor (Bhutan and Ethiopia) to reasonably affluent (Greece, Kuwait, the Republic of Korea and Singapore.)

(Programme on Empowerment of Women" compiled by Institute of Secretariat Training and Management)

The undervaluation of woman is mainly due to the deliberate, conspitorial undervaluation of her work, ability, talent and skill. Of men's total work time in industrial nations, roughly two-thirds is spent in paid activities and one-third in unpaid activities. If women's unpaid work were properly valued it is quite possible that women would emerge, in most societies, as the major bread-winners since they put in longer hours of work than men. The total number and quantity of work done by women are also much greater. Women, working at both home and outside, work almost double of men. Such a revaluation will effect a radical shift in women's economic and social positions. Wives, then, will have an entitlement to family-income, rather than wives depending on an act of benevolence from their patriarchs.

In Bangladesh, for example, men and women were found to work approximately the same number of hours per week, but men devoted 90% of their work hours to income-generating activities and women had to allocate 80% of their work time to unpaid, unappreciated household chores. Work, in the latter category, are not evaluated as productive or income-generative, although it will be impossible for men to work or generate income if not for this support from his family and household. What a strange irony it is that the support-base for a productive,income-generating work is considered unproductive and valueless!

Power is enjoyed in proportion to the evaluation of work in money terms. Because women have less or no money in hand and since major part of their work does not generate money-income, they have little or no say in the allocation or spending of family income; they have no part in family/household decisions - not even with regard to their own children, however though they take all the pain and responsibility for bringing them up! Argentine women work, on an average, 73 hours a week at home if they are not employed outside, and 56 hours if they are. But in most economically backward countries, women's household work do not decrease with her employment outside; so, she starts working many more number of hours.

Table 2: **Percentage of Economically Active Population**

Census	Male	Female
1901	61.11	31.70
1911	61.90	33.73
1921	60.52	32.67
1931	58.27	27.63
1941	DNA	DNA
1951	54.05	23.30
1961	57.10	37.96
1971	52.75	14.15
1981	52.65	19.76

The table above reveals that the work- participation rates have been falling since last half century, both for males and females.

(Women and Empowerment, ISTM)

Traditional economic activities, which have traditionally provided employment to women, have suffered in competition to the more advanced technologies. Home-based women worker or those working in the highly exploitative unorganized sector, do not get the protective coverage of the labour laws.

The present crisis of fuel and water due to the development/degradation programmes, has further increased the burden/workload on women. There are above 30 percent of rural households, headed by women, who bear all the heavy burden of earning and taking care of their families; in addition, these women also suffer due to lack of access to the means of production and the ownership of land and other property. Their unequal and inequitable status, their physical and economic hardship get worse due to the fact that neither the society nor the women themselves perceive their role in society as anything but marginal; the women themselves fail to put value to their work (which is highly significant for the very survival of their families, and even the society) This misperception is because the man is always regarded as the bread-winner and the woman goes *out* to earn only when the man's /family's income is not enough. Value is attached only to that category of work which allows money in return. That is why when a woman earns half of what man does, her work is assessed as half efficient or half productive, though it is actually not so. Sometimes, it may be true that women are not equally efficient since they do not get the right opportunities to acquire skills - particularly technical skills.

Over their lifetime, women change their employment status more often than men do. They are also likely to be self-employed or employed in occupations with flexible hours, such as "sub-contracted" domestic work. Women everywhere — in both developed and developing world - are less likely to be in the organized labour force, or in any position of power and responsibility.

In almost all societies, women receive less for their work, receive less opportunities to education and development of vocational skills, have less control of natural, household and monetary resources, have also less access to better paying jobs and promotions and therefore, almost no power (Inequalities are not merely between men and women, but also between ethnic, religious and caste groups and across the regions). There is an increasing demand for female labour in the unorganized sector because it is profitable for the manufactures to get work done at a much lower cost. In the organized sector demand is less as they have to abide by the service rules and laws laid down by the Factory Acts.

In India, women's real wages are 51 percent of men's and only 34% of the cases can be explained by the fact of being "less qualified." Women are less qualified because they have less opportunities to acquire skills or get qualified. In Kenya, for example, women get 18% lower than men, even after adjusting for skill and experience. In most countries of Latin America female wages are 71% of average male wages and only 20% can be explained in terms of differences in human capital. Even in former Soviet Union women earned 30% less than men. Weaker labour- market opportunities produce weaker incentives to educate girls. This creates a vicious cycle since less educated women are much less likely to educate their daughters. While women desire more of cash-income activities, their ability to do so is limited by the same forces which are pushing them towards it.

TABLE 3: **Female Wages Are Lower Than Male Wages, but This is Changing**

Country	First observation	Average Second observation	annual percentage change
Brazil	50.2 (1981)	53.6 (1990)	0.7
Colombia	67.2 (1984)	70.2 (1990)	0.7
Cote d'Ivoire	75.7 (1985)	81.4 (1988)	2.4
Indonesia	55.6 (1986)	60.0 (1992)	1.3
Philippines	70.9 (1978)	80.0 (1988)	1.2
Thailand	73.5 (1980)	79.8 (1990)	0.8

Note: Monthly earnings for Indonesia and Thailand, rural and urban; for all others, urban only.

Source: Tzannatos

Importance of Education

Popular education or the literacy campaigns (particularly in West Bengal and Maharashtra) aims at developing a critical awareness, among the marginalised and the oppressed groups, about their situation and what they can do to improve upon. It also seeks to effect a radical change in their behaviour and attitudes so that they can acquire the confidence to challenge the oppressive situations and structures. As the experiences of Latin America, South Africa and, of course, of our own nation shows, popular education hits at oppression or oppressive system without being gender-specific. Like in case of pre-Mandela South Africa, popular or people's education was "oppositional" in purpose and content - oppositional to the "power-privilege axis," of course.

Education enables both men and women to acquire basic skills and ability and therefore, education is the most important instrument for human resource development. Education is also taken (by policy-makers) as a tool for bringing about social equality and upliftment. It is believed, "if we are educating a man, we are educating an individual; if we are educating a woman, we are educating the entire family." A World Bank booklet very rightly says, "moving towards gender equality means moving from argument to action."

> *"Man's knowledge depends mainly on his activity in material production, through which he comes gradually to understand the phenomena, the properties and the laws of nature, and the relations between himself and nature; and through his activity in production he also gradually comes to understand, in varying degrees, certain relations that exist between man and man."* — *Mao Zedong*

11

Women's Work and Migration

Migration provides an excellent example of the way women's activities - even if productive in the traditional sense - can appear to be almost invisible to policy-makers and researchers. Women move from her parents' home/area/ country/society due to her marriage; thus marital migration constitutes a majority of all the migratory moves, and affects a woman's life and status in a major way. This is one form of migration which is never taken into consideration because that affects women only. It is of no concern even to the women researchers or social workers or policy makers because they, unconsciously are conditioned by the values, beliefs and necessities of the patriarchal and patrilocal world! The paradox is that marital migration is the most destructive form of migration for women - it destroys her identity as an individual and establishes her firmly as an instrument for reproduction and submissive service only. If marital migration is questioned then the very structure of patriarchy will be questioned, if patriarchy is being questioned, then the very structure of capitalism (or exploitation-oriented socio-economic structure) will be questioned and if capitalism and patriarchy both are questioned, we do not need to question anythingelse. There will be no oppression or inequality.

In recent years the Chinese government has encouraged late marriage and tried to control the unhealthy craze for a male child by making one-child family mandatory. One cannot change a society or social beliefs and superstitions by the stroke of a law; so this enactment has, naturally, led to increase in female foeticide and female infanticide. But this also has managed to shake the patrilocal system to a certain extent. If that one child is female then the husband has to move over to the wife's family/residence, because it is mandatory for a Chinese citizen to take care of his/her parents in their old age. The Philippines society traditionally makes it obligatory for the daughters (even if married) to take care of their aged/retired parents.

According to Lotika Menon, prior to 1970s nine out of ten studies on migration were restricted to the cause and effects of male migration, and even that one out of ten devoted less than 5 per cent of its pages to the problems related to female migration. Very little is known about the role of women in the decisions to migrate or to stay behind. The following is an interesting peep into the types of migrants and the motives/reasons behind their migration.

Very few studies have asked women why they "chose" to move. (Did they really have the freedom to "choose"?). They do not seem to have been asked, "who played the crucial role in the decision to move - you or your husband? or "Did you consider the possibility of your husband only migrating? Why/Why not."

Table 4.1 **Types of Female Migration**

	Types of Migrant and Motive	Country	Source
1.	Young Girls with parents	General	Yousself et al. 1979
2.	Girls alone for education	Ghana	Caldwell, 1969
		Ivory Coast	Roussel 1970
		Solomon Islands	Chapman 1976
3.	Young unmarried women to work as domestic servants	Latin America	Smith, 1973 Jelin, 1977
	(i) as factory workers	Malaysia	Ariffin 1978
		Oceania	Haman, 1978
	(ii) as prostitutes	Indonesia	Papanek, 1975
	(iii) as prostitutes (divorcees)	Nigeria	Cohen, 1969
4.	Young unmarried women in search of adventure	West Africa	Little 1973
	in search of households	Oceania	Stanhope, and Prior, 1977
5.	Unmarried mothers	Uganda	Obbo, 1975
			Nelson 1979
6.	Marital Migration	Cameroon	Podlewski, 1975
		India	Majumder, 1977
			Libbee and Sopher, 1975
7.	Married women moving with husbands	India	Singh, 1978
		Iran	Bauer, 1979
		New Guinea	Oueser, 1969
8.	Married women alone		
	(i) as servants	Niger Diarra,	1974
	(ii) as traders	Nigeria, Ghana	Sudarkasa, 1977
			Nadel, 1942
	(iii) for childbirth	Papua New Guinea	Young, 1977

9.	Widows and Divorcees	India	Committee on the Status of Women 1974
		Malaysia	Strange, 1976
10.	Grandmothers as child minders	Oceania	Stanhope and prior, 1977
11.	Circulating women	Hong Kong	
		Malaysia	Strauch, 1979
12.	Nomads	Australia	Gale, 1974
		Iran	Beck, 1978
		West Africa	Riesman, 1974
13.	Refugees	General	UN High Commissioner 1980

Boserup's study tells us that the large-scale migration of young women to the towns of Latin America (like in case of India) results from the fact that "poor farmers" (mostly scheduled castes and scheduled tribes in India) "send their daughters to towns" "to become domestic servants, because they are not needed at home if the mother does a little more than her own share of domestic work".

One important question is whether autonomous female migration is a cause or a consequence of the liberation of these doubly underprivileged women. In the Ivory Coast, amongst the Baoule, for example, women migrate as an act of defiance and outnumber men in the migration flow. Is it so in case of the young tribal women in our study, or does the argument of Boserup hold good? The main reason why domestic service is such a popular occupation for women migrants is the fact that 'live-in domestics' are under the protection of their employers 24 hours a day and thereby enjoy good food, good clothes and lot of comforts that are inseparable parts of upper-class urban iife.

Education is a liberating factor itself. But there is less scope for educated girls to do anything productive or income-generative in the under developed areas they necessarily come from. The greater the degree of discrimination against women in matters of employment and wages, the less is the livelihood apportunities of migrant women. When they have no choice but to migrate, they opt for the job of domestic workers. Marital migration for women holds a special significance. Men can improve their socio-economic status by acquiring higher or specilised education or by getting better job; women can achieve this by "marrying well", or, in other words, by marrying a man of the status she aspires to.

Latin America is one region of the developing world where females clearly predominate the rural-urban migration scene. An extreme case of female pre-dominance can be found in Chile where migrants to Santiago, aged 15-24, included only 64 males for every 100 females, and almost all the women work in the cities as domestic workers. There were some 90,000 female domestic workers in the Peruvian capital in 1966-67. At older ages female migration responds more to family obligations than to direct economic factors. In 1971 in Indonesia, for example, 66 per cent of female migration (aged 15-19) to the capital was for the service sector; the corresponding figure for Thailand was 70 per cent, and for Philippines 80 per cent. 1971 census of India showed 82 males per 100 females in intra-district moves, 104 in inter-district moves and 142 in inter-state moves. To medium-sized towns, male and female migrants are almost of equal number, but males outnumber females in case of migration to the metropolitan cities. One study on Delhi (conducted in 1977) showed that 81 per cent of the female migrants or settlers cited poverty or other economic problems as the cause, though family, kinship and caste were major considerations while deciding the destination of the "move". 72 per cent of male migrants were literate whereas only 47 per cent of the female migrants, who were working, were literate, and only 65 per cent of the women migrants could get a job....But that job, as we all know, was underpaid; the excuse offered was stereotyped, viz: women are illiterate, uneducated, untrained and, therefore, unskilled!....It is a widely accepted common observation that a woman is underpaid even if she is doing exactly the same work as her male counterpart. Semi-skilled and skilled occupations usually involve personal apprenticeships and a degree of independence which are available to men and usually not to women in such a highly sex-segregated society.

Education or vocational training of the girls are neglected or avoided by the economically backward families due to two reasons. First, the parents do not think it wise to spend their very limited monetary and other resources on the education of their daughters as the money return of this kind of financial investment will be not to them, but to the daughters'in-laws. Secondly, they fear that they will not be able to afford the dowry for an appropriate husband who needs to be better educated / qualified than his wife. Thirdly, education, specially higher education and training in skill-development give a sense of confidence, independence and a courage to protest and defy. No patriarchal society - not even the females within that system - can tolerate that in a female. We have seen (in the present study) how education, and later migration away from the shackles of family and community traditions, plus independent earning and living have ignited the flame of consciousness among our respondents. Marital migration, for example, takes full care to ensure that such consciousness can never be ignited or raised. Two daughters will not be allowed to go, in marriage, to the same family- not even to the same village. Even two girls from village A will not be allowed to be married in village B. The slightest opportunity for sharing thoughts and feeling - not to speak of some kind of solidarity - is denied by religious and customary laws. The brides have to be strangers to the new set-up and got to live with strangers only for the rest of their lives. The wife is further disadvantaged as she hardly ever gets a chance to know her husband and to be known .....the couple is seldom allowed any private space or time. Thus, one way in which migration may contribute to improving the status of women is by helping to snap the links with the husbands family. Life away from these kinds of constraints allows the woman to develop a kind of "camaraderie" (or, intimacy) with her husband; this, in turn, offers her a role in the family decision-making.

She may, even, get an opportunity to re-establish relationship with her parental family. In Bolivia, both migrant and non-migrant women in areas of high male-migration, gained increased control over economic resources, which is followed by greater access to public life, in general. Dominican women migrate to USA as domestic workers, sex-workers or workers in exploitative garment factories, but opportunities available for autonomy are there. Urbanization also may improve their status.

Even migration of men only can improve the status of women who are left behind. Women, then, have to manage the land left behind by their husbands and brothers; they, even, have to take decisions. She may get regular money from her better-earning husband.

The causes and effect of migration are different for the rich and the poor, or, rather, for the "have" and the "have-not". A man belonging to the rural elite (which is composed of higher castes and powerful peasantry) migrates to the city for advanced education and subsequently to take up an urban job, thus adding to the family's income and his "status." He builds the capitalist base to agriculture. On the other hand, poorest peasants, dispossessed tenants, landless labourers and artisans whose crafts are not valued anymore, migrate in order to avoid underemployment or to get proper employment. Women suffer due to both kinds of migration. Elite class women suffer emotionally because of physical separation from husband and the greater control over her activities by the other patriarchs. She can be relatively free and demanding with her husband. Poor women bear, in addition to the emotional problems (though such sentiments and emotions are more a privilege of leisure and luxury), the increased burden of not only looking after the home and children, but also of supporting the family. Very often they also have to look for employment because the money their husbands send home is never enough. He is underpaid as he invariably ends up in the unorganized sector, totally unprotected by law; he has to cope up with city-living where cost of living is much higher than in the villages or in the small towns; besides, he may also become a victim of typical vices associated with city-life and the lonely and frustrated life of somebody uprooted and distanced from his family. Often the women who stay back, have to undergo exploitation and harassment in the hands of the affluent locals who are the sole providers of work. Efforts at self-employment and self-reliance meet with no success because of lack of capital for investment, absence of training and marketing facilities and no legal protection whatsoever. Such women-workers go un-noticed because of their low-paid, low-prestige work in the unorganized/unprotected sector. Only 12 per cent of them are allowed to work in the organized sector. A global study puts woman-headed households in India at 18.7 per cent. The reasons are not encouraging for women. Many households are women-headed not because matriarchy is being recognized, nor because women are allowed to be independent, but because these are households of widows, divorcees and the deserted women (where men have not allowed them freedom which can give them position of honour and power, but have only given up their own responsibilities). No study takes into account, separately or specially, those households which are woman-headed because of male migrations - as if male-migration is of no consequence in the life of a woman. Delhi seems to be hosting the highest number of migrant population and the states of Kerala, Uttar Pradesh, Bihar and Jammu and Kashmir are the main exporters of such hapless population.

Interestingly some view male migration from rural to urban as a blessing, because that, apparently, takes away the pressure from land. Little do they observe that migration actually is the result of pressure on land due to diminishing agricultural land area and that diminution is due to the "development" projects and unplanned industrialization. Industrialization seldom helps women, because neither their families nor their society provide them with the opportunities or resources to acquire or develop skills. Female-specific traditional skills get less in demand. The general pattern of the social life is derived from the "ideology of dependence" and the notion of the "social inferiority" of the female - sanctified by the scriptures and supported by the folklore and tradition. Three decades after independence, the Committee on the Status of Women observed that there was a "national neglect of women"; it used socio-economic indicators like sex-ratio in population and mortality rates of female babies & mothers, literacy and education, employment, wages, access to health services, etc.

In 20 years, between 1951 and 1971, the population of Delhi nearly tripled. Delhi accounts for only 3 per cent of country's population but 11 per cent of the inter-state migrants! Male migrants are slightly in majority.

Statistical Profile of Migrants

	Number of Migrants	Years in the city			
		Up to 5	5 to 10	10-20	above 20
Caste					
Peasants	57	2	15	23	17
Scheduledcastes	37	13	12	6	6
Others	3	-	2	1	-
Total	97	15	29	30	23
Principal Occupation of the family					
Cultivation	46	6	11	9	20
Agricultural labour	45	6	16	20	3
Traditional	6	3	2	1	-
Total	97	15	29	30	23
Operational holding (hectares)					
None	27	5	9	10	3
Less than 1	35	6	11	13	5
1-2	23	4	3	4	12
2 and above	12	-	6	3	3
Total	97	15	29	30	23
Age Group					
20-25	13	12	1	-	-

25-30	30	3	26	1	-
30-35	16	-	2	14	-
35-40	13	-	-	12	1
40-45	20	-	-	3	17
45-50	4	-	-	-	4
50-55	1	-	-	-	1
Total	97	15	29	30	23
Education					
Illiterate	71	6	20	25	20
Primary	18	3	7	5	3
Secondary	6	4	2	-	-
College	2	2	-	-	-
Total	97	15	29	30	23
Status before migration					
Student	8	8	-	-	-
Farmer, Craftsman	36	1	7	11	17
Wage earner	39	2	12	19	6
Jobless	14	4	10	-	-
Total	97	15	29	30	23

By whom advised to come to city					
Village friend	17	-	3	12	2
Father	11	7	4	-	-
Relative	43	8	18	10	7
Own decision	26	-	4	8	14
Total	97	15	29	30	23
With whom came to city					
Village friend	15	-	7	6	2
Father	11	7	4	-	-
Relative	50	8	18	15	9
Other person	21	-	-	9	12
Total	97	15	29	30	23
With whom stayed in the city					
Village fellow	20	-	8	10	2
Father	11	7	4	-	-
Relative	41	8	17	11	5
Own arrangement	25	-	-	9	16
Total	97	15	29	30	23
Amount earned (Rs)					
Less than 200	6	4	2	-	-
200-250	26	9	8	5	4
250-300	36	1	9	14	12
Above 300	29	1	10	11	7
Total	97	15	29	30	23

Amount sent home (Rs)					
Nothing	17	8	4	3	2
Upto 10	50	38	4	12	12
50-100	25	3	8	9	5
100 and above	17	-	5	6	6
Total	97	15	29	30	23
Attitude towards present job					
Happy	61	15	20	16	10
Partially Happy	15	-	7	4	4
Satisfied	11	-	2	3	6
Do not mind	10	-	-	7	3
Total	97	15	29	30	23
Frequency of visits to village					
No visit	14	12	1	-	1
Once a year	7	-	-	4	3
Twice a year	19	-	5	10	4
Three times a year	57	3	23	16	15
Total	97	15	29	30	23
Plans for the future					
Permanent return to					
Village	67	5	15	27	20
Do not Know	26	10	14	2	-
Bring family to city	4	-	-	1	3
Total	97	15	29	30	23

Source : Our own surveys & interviews.

A sociological study of 728 working mothers in USA revealed that

29% worked because "my husband is not earning enough"

22% worked because "my husband is dead"

14% worked because "my husband is sick"

13% worked because "my husband left me"

11% worked because "my husband could not support me"

11% worked because "I would rather work".

i.e. 89% worked due to economic neccessity.

The situation is quite similar in India (the statistics, of course, cannot be the same). (National Planning Committee, "Women's role in Planned Economy")

In India, the reasons behind women taking up gainful employment are, broadly, like this -

1) family-oriented economic reasons (even if not hardship)
2) striving towards self-fulfillment and emancipation, and
3) desire to use one's qualifications and leisure time.

The women in the first category may belong to the economically higher stratum even (though the overwhelming majority are from the middle, low and no-income groups. Widowed, divorced, deserted and unmarried women are more likely to go for income-generating activities. Some of the unmarried girls may want to earn with the purpose of saving for her own dowry!.

At this stage, a comparison of the position of women, with regard to her work with a few societies of both the developed and developing world, can be quite indicative and supportive of our experience and view-point. We find women and women- workers remain discriminated even if the people in general are emancipated and empowered on the socio-economic plane.

Not so long ago, Dutch women, for example, were only housewives and, therefore, their work and contribution to national productivity were totally unrecognised. In the Netherlands 15 years ago, 32% of all women over the age of 18 were in paid employment. Now the figure is 56% in comparison to 70% for men, 90% of men have a full-time job and 1% work less than 12 hours a week. 35% of women have full time job and 15% work less than 12 hours a week. Women earn less than men (average gross annual income for men is Dfl 40,500 while women earn Dfl 21,000). This difference results from the large number of part-time jobs women are engaged in and the difference in the average hourly pay; women earn Dfl 21 per hour, men earn Dfl 29 per hour. The difference in gross hourly pay is also due to the fact that women hold lower positions because they have less training and because by working part-time, they have fever chances of promotion. They are also less experienced because many leave paid employment for a number of years to take care of their children. However, these reasons do not completely explain the difference in payment. There appears to be discrimination. As a contrast, we can take Peoples' Republic of China's example, where would-be-mothers are allowed a very long leave (as suggested by doctor) and nursing mothers are allowed to work part-time on full salary/wages. Similar benefits women in China enjoy if they have to take care of aged parents..

Women are increasingly working outside the home, but only 20% of women earn enough to be able to live independently. Thus even after divorce, many women are dependent on alimony or a social welfare assistance— a minimum benefit paid by the authorities in the Netherlands to those who cannot earn that amount themselves. The benefit paid is extremely limited and it is almost impossible to keep a family on this amount. It is possible to earn a little extra, but according to strict rules. Many women work as substitute workers, home helps or for an employment agency in insecure circumstances. Their employment contract is frequently temporary.

Moreover, increasing participation by women in the labour market does not mean equality has been achieved in the relationships between men and women on the labour market and in the field of career. There are still many 'male' and 'female' careers. Men are making inroads in women's careers and often make a career for themselves at the expense of women, as in education and health care. Women in men's jobs are still a rarity. In education, too, there are still discriminations. Girls, on average, choose a lower career and, more often, a caring profession. Science and technology are still not very popular among girls.

Care, which women have to take of their home, children and the elderly is totally unrecognised and unpaid. Women, not in employment, spend an average of 26 hours a week on housework,while women in paid employment spend 16 hours. In all cases, men spend about 10 hours on household responsibilities whether their wives work or not. This has remained the same as ten years ago. Women in paid employment, therefore, still bear a double burden.

In El Salvador, armed conflict, deportation, resultant economic crisis and migration have led to a steady rise in the female-headed households. Thirty nine percent families are headed by a female. Women are increasingly responsible for family income, a role which was previously reserved for men. It is becoming rarer, in the countryside as well as in the city, to find women who are exclusively housewives. Even when the man is present, she contributes in all kinds of ways to the family income. Role change for women results from the absence of the man or because he cannot or will not fulfil the role of protector and breadwinner.

Women are increasingly present in the formal labour market. They work , primarily, in trade and services. About 63% and 53% respectively, of total labour in this sector is accounted for by women. In industry, the figure is 44%. In domestic service only 3% is accounted for by men. Most economically active women (60%) work in the informal sector. Despite the significant increase in participation in the labour market women's economic position has not automatically improved, because their income is significantly lower than men's. Their work is valued much lower financially.

At the political level, the women's movement plays an important role in a number of processes: national reconstruction, democratic elections, defence of women's rights, legal changes and revisions etc. The aim is to bring about positive change for women. The women's movement, directly and indirectly, supports the efforts of grassroot- women to improve their circumstances. Everything around indicate that women are in the process of giving a new form to their identity. Men are resisting the 'process'or are trying to avoid it.

The most important activities of the Women's Unions in recent years have been aimed at the provision of credit and training with a strong impact on development. The most urgent need is to link this credit to productive activities to ensure that female borrowers do not come under even more pressure. Relationships must be forged between credit and the establishment of savings systems.

Many of the other activities of the Women's Union are connected with the practical needs of women and are based on women's traditional tasks in the community and the family. Women are particularly active in the community in forming production teams, establishing savings groups, rotating funds, community emergency funds, training centres etc.

It is mainly men who become involved in development programmes as primary spokesmen and representatives of the families. This does not do justice to women. Women are not mere extensions of men; they have their own needs, wishes and priorities; they want to progress, gain esteem, some influence and control over their own lives and the lives of their families. However, it is now evident that the problem associated with the relationships between men and women cannot be solved by working with women in isolation, without taking into consideration men, their families and the community. The imbalances in these relationship prevent women from standing up for their own rights. Solving this is a crucial issue for both the parties.

There is an urgent need to make men, and even women, gender sensitive and to train them in this respect. "Women, at local, regional, national and international levels, must organize to demand their economic, political and cultural inheritance and to raise their status, so that equality can be constructed". (Sister Rosily, Holy Cross Social Service, India)

Development model, which India adopted in the post-independence period, was apparently aimed at achieving long-term goal of a welfare State through redistribution of wealth and income-opportunities. A series of very effective labour laws were enacted; but hardly ever, those were strictly enforced....the immense possibility of most labour operating, or rather being forced to operate, outside the jurisdiction of these laws was not given any thought. The planners forgot that a poverty and problem stricken economy of a Third

World can not work within the frame-work evolved for a fully developed economy! Agricultural/commercial farms and firms, both, increasingly preferred employing "flexible" labour, which could be disposed off without having to bother about the labour laws and the welfare provisions stipulated in these. This advantage that factory-owners and the various other types of employers enjoyed led to the rise in the use of casual, temporary and contract labour. Since women were underpaid, i.e. since female labour was cheaper than male labour, there was a growing preference for female labour. With the adoption of the New Economic Policy (1991), the stress was on improving skill and efficiency and make production cost-effective. Thus women, whose labour mostly is unskilled and not trained for that level of technology, got exposed to greater vulnerability. Women and children get increasingly absorbed in jobs which can be described as "precarious". The structural adjustment policy package entails deflation, devaluation, deregulation and decentralization" (Jha and Pujari, "Indian Women Today" 1996)

Deflationary policies and trends force many poor women in urban India to fend for themselves as self-employed in the labour market. Devaluation, due to trade liberalization, increased demand for female labour, particularly in the export industries. The kind of employment offered is low-paid and with no security. Deregulation and decentralization of domestic industrial production create "flexible" female labour which is intermittently employed and that, too, on low wages. Those, who did not get even this much of an un-enviable opportunity, took to menial kind of self-employment as petty traders or vendors or even as rag-pickers. Women's work is, thus, not only outside the purview of the labour legislation but even outside the physical and moral protection that family, community or caste can provide. An extremely notable point is that the employers preferred or selected those who were untrained and trainable and not those who were already trained. This may sound unprofessional, but this benefitted the employers best..... they could make maximum (or should we say "excess") profit, then. Obviously, it was much easier to exploit and pay low wages to a totally untrained person. Morally it looks less objectionable and the employee is too nervous, diffident and insecure to demand fair wages. Such gross injustice to women as a class is possible also because of the "cultural" notions about "man's job" and "woman's job". Most countries outside India think that a woman cannot be or should not be an assistant to a male brick-layer (for example) and men in most European countries would not think of being a typist or a stenographer. In the labour markets of the industrialized countries, the sharp distinction between "male" and "female" tasks goes together with a hierarchical ordering so that women perform the jobs requiring least qualifications and maximum supervision; supervision, needless to remind our readers, is invariably by men who are either really more qualified or deemed to be more qualified.....It may not be all that meaningless to ask, at this juncture, at what stage of economic development a change takes place from "age-hierarchy" to "sex-hierarchy". This was the most gender hostile development in the history of mankind. This seems to have happened when productive activities moved from the premises of "where the family lived" to a specialized working place - a workshop or a shop, for example.

The transfer of production from the home to specialized premises is not the only explanation for the change in women's status in the labour market; inferior position of girls and young women in the education system, and specially in vocational training, is as significant an explanation. But, at the same time, we cannot ignore the fact that among the Middle Class, educated girls are more in demand in the marriage market. The rising prices and increasing economic hardships weaken the patriarchal position of the male members....... women are allowed to - even expected to - work and bring extra income to the family. It can also happen that the dowry demand will be less (in case of a highly educated, earning girl). Thirdly, the stereo-typical notions and cultural beliefs and bias against woman are created through literature, audio-visuals, other forms of media and even through school text-books-not merely through age-old social and religious beliefs and superstitions. Women, thus, start believing, from their girlhood only, that they are inferior to men both in physical and intellectual abilities. So, they tutor themselves to quietly accept their blatantly discriminatory position in the labour market.

While there are nearly 42 million more male cultivators than women, there are 6 million more female labourers than cultivators. There is no record of those who worked as agricultural labour in their own field or as domestic workers in their own homes or in a large joint family.

Women workers in the organized sector have been among the first to be shunted out under the garb of "voluntary retirement scheme". A 55 year old deserted woman, for example, who used to be a machine - operator at a monthly wage of Rs. 2,000 per month (a ridiculously low wage for this kind of a skilled job) had no option but to work as a sweeper in a private creche earning only Rs 400/- a month. The process of economic development should actually be a process of expanding the capabilities of people. But it does not happen that way— especially not in case of women, the dalits and the tribals, the most backward and discriminated.

Like in Nature, in social life and economic system also, every force released has a momentum which, perhaps, cannot be regulated. Once the process of exploitation starts, it goes on and on and gets worse and worse, till it becomes so bad and unbearable that the exploited start feeling "we have nothing to lose but our chains" and thus the momentum of an opposite force sets in. To contain that

(1) a declining trend in employment for adult women.

(2) an increase in employment of adolescent girls, and

(3) an increase in employment of girl children starts. Younger the exploited, meeker she is and more scared to defy or protest.

In 1921, the year of the non-cooperation movement, over 39 million women or one third of the total female population were in the workforce— 68,000 were in medical profession (mainly nurses or even non-skilled assistants), 30,000 in education and scientific fields (not necessarily as fully trained or professionals) and 6,000 in law and business.....Domestic workers numbered 737,000. The last still, is the most advised and sought after occupation for women till this day. The reasons are very simple... women are taken to be best and good only in domestic work. Unskilled women also prefer it as among the exploitative occupations, this is most remunerative.The workers do not have to spend for their boarding and lodging.

The first cotton and jute mill, established in 1850's employed women, but accurate records were not available till 1911. About 1 lakh of them were working in the textile factories of the Bombay province. About 75 per cent of them worked full time, the rest were employed casually, on daily basis i.e. whenever production accelerated. Women were never allotted the skilled or creative job of weaving.The other biases are that women are never allowed to lay the bricks with her own hands, however much she is working along with the male mason, and women are prohibited from ploughing or even touching the plough, though all other heavy work are done by them. They were made to slog with the tedious and mentally unrewarding job of cleaning the cotton, winding and reeling the thread,etc. About 14,000 women were engaged in similar kind of unrewarding jobs in the Bengal jute mills. In 1928, about 250,000 women worked in factories (mostly cotton and jute mills).

Another 250,000 worked in tea-gardens constituting 27 per cent of the total working force. About 30,000 to 40,000 worked in the Bombay brothels. The most disturbing statistics is that as many as 78,000 women had to work in the mines (later, in 1957, prohibited by the Mines Act).

During the last quarter of the 19th century, factory legislations, designed to improve working conditions for women, received attention from many quarters. About the same time Lord Shafetsbury drew the governments attention to factory working conditions in England, Maj. Moore wrote a report on the conditions in the Bombay factories, and Mr J A Ballard particularly pointed to the acute hardship faced by women and children in the Indian factories. A seven-member government- appointed committee (all men — three English and four Indians) reviewed the situation and, by a majority vote (surprisingly it was not unanimous), declared legislation unnecessary. Two men, both English, had called for "regulatory reforms" and in return, they were bantered as "ignorant English philanthropists". They were trying to raise the wages or the cost of labour.

Despite local hostility to legislation, India had its first Factory Act by 1881. Ten years later, an amendment limited the total daily working hours of women to eleven, and 20 years after that (in 1911) employers were not allowed to make women work at night. The most note-worthy part of the story is all these initiatives came from the ruling country (viz. England) and not from the Indian philanthropists or reformers. The workers themselves had not raised any such demand!

A series of international conferences viz: in Berlin (1890), Paris (1900) and Berne (1905), tried to define minimum working conditions suitable, or rather, favourable for workers (men and women) of all the countries. The 1919 International Labour Conference in Washington D.C. stimulated further conventions. The International Labour Organization (ILO), composed of the eight most important countries of the world, was established at this meeting.

The Factory Act (1948) restricted the working hours of women to 54 hours a week.... approximately 9 hours a day, and they could not be made to work at night, i.e. not before 6 a.m. and not after 7 p.m. The Mines Act (1957) demanded that women cannot be made to lift weight heavier than 65 pounds. Women were not allowed to work underground. The Plantation Labour Act provided maternity benefits like free medical treatment and even a maternity bonus. Provision of creche and free time to nursing mothers to breastfeed their babies is obligatory for the employers. But no such provision or legal protection is available to those who work in the unorganized sector.

The All India women's Conference (AIWC), while organizing women in the unorganized sector, laid continuous stress on legislation. It demanded that ILO should have a female representative (of the workers, obviously,) from India. AIWC kept on demanding social insurance, maternity benefits and other measures to improve the working conditions of women. Rajkumari Amrit Kaur, on the other hand, was not all that wrong in warning that special legislations for women would make employers lay off women workers and hire men, instead. Exactly that has happened—women are being increasingly shunted out of organized sector..... Even in agriculture the number of male farmers is rising and the number of female labour is falling. The pathetic irony is that the women, themselves, do not want these legal restrictions on their working 'time'. They would rather, work and earn all the time — till the birth of the child actually takes place, and even in extremely dangerous situations, like underground in a mine. They live too much below the poverty line to afford any privilege or enjoy any rights. Laws, in any case, are only on paper, and are hardly ever implemented or enforced. In most cases, the enforcing authorities take illegal money from the exploiters. Even the tribunals or labour courts are not sensitized enough to feel for the have-nots, which include women.

Women's lives in India and the world over are circumscribed by what can be termed as the "five P's", viz (1) patriarchy, (2) productive resources - access - inadequacy, (3) poverty, (4) promotion & advancement - insufficiency and (5) powerlessness. "Gender relationship of dominance and subordination is a political relationship which derives material sustenance from conditions and structures of production and its legitimacy from a tradition/culture which upholds subordination of women". (A Peggy and B Judith — "Women's Perspectives: Towards an Ethical, Equitable, Just and Sustainable Development"—ISIS International issue, 1993). "A radical change in the attitudes of women, induced by an awareness of their rights, which are constitutionally guaranteed and legally protected, will be/should be the first step in the complex process of transforming the social structure so that women may enjoy full equality with men in every sphere of life" (Umashankar Jha and Premlata Pujari - 'Indian Women Today: tradition, modernity and challenge", vol.I, 1996)

Conclusion

The tribal situation in India has been a victim of "whims and fancy" (to say the least) of various regimes— both colonial and post-colonial (Shalini Mehta - "Continuity and Change Among the Tribals" in Miri (ed.), "Continuity and Change in Tribal Society" (1993). British administrators-turned ethnographers and anthropologist treated tribal communities as isolates, tribals as noble savages. The deterioration of tribal communities was attributed to the Sanskritization of semi-tribal chiefs and to the vulnerability of tribal character. We have discussed on many occasions before that tribal nature is a mixture of conservatism—a deeprooted, difficult-to-change love for its own culture and tradition — with a powerful urge for modernity and all the benefits associated with it. This is an important reason why the tribals score better than the Scheduled castes if given an opportunity. With the end of the colonial system, there were vigorous attempts to bring the tribal society into the mainstream of the new administrative set-up, policy and programmes. This, obviously, put an end to the political dominance of the tribes in their own region and they were roped into a new system of production relations.

The resource-base and the social and cultural heritage of the tribal population are getting eroded through a combination of development interventions, commercial exploitation and ineffective legal and administrative systems. However much it was realized and accepted that elimination of exploitation should be a major strategy for tribal development, it was not accorded any priority. Land alienation, unjust excise and forest policies are the various avenues of exploitation. Wherever new development is taking place in tribal areas, the people there are losing their own land in return of some monetary compensation; but the amount is insufficient, just symbolic. But the most important factor in this context is that money cannot take the place of land. Its productivity is neither recurrent nor permanent, spreading over generations. Besides, money has no meaning and no value in tribal economy and tribal system of production. Not only are they deprived of their land and forest, the tribals are also being constantly pushed back from wherever new opportunities are arising. They are also pushed back by the new migrants. They are thrown into the bottom substructure of the new socio-economic system. The tribals are the hapless victims of the new eco-political order.

A community and its elements are always in the process of incessant change, although at varying degrees. Struggle for justice, equality and independence, are inherent in the very nature of its structure. Latent or manifest, woman's struggle constitutes an essential element of the male-dominated family and social life. "When women participate with total commitment for change and social justice and in that process structural changes take place, the inherent strength and importance of women can be enhanced." (Devasia- "Empowering Women for Sustainable Development.") Complete and all-pervasive development of woman is impossible without social justice. It protects her as it limits the power of man and does away with his privileges. Social justice must -

1) safeguard the independence of woman-her position, opinion and decision,
2) provide equality of opportunity to woman
3) include provisions for the utilization of woman's potentialities,
4) include economic, social, cultural and political aspects of a woman's life

Social justice, thus, is an essential pre-condition to development.

Development is not merely the upliftment of the standard of life of the poor, but - more importantly - protection of the general population from getting exploited, oppressed and poorer. An understanding of the nature of existing economic opportunities, associated labour market forces and the nature and attitude of the deprived (like the adivasis and the women) is essential. So programme on attitudinal changes is of much significance in the developmental projects. These can be like the following:

a) Programmes which should have direct impact on the lives of women.
b) Programmes which meet the felt needs of women.
c) Programmes that would enable them to perceive their needs.
d) Programmes that would ultimately lead to self help activities.
e) Programmes that would help them to integrate with the main stream of the society (i.e. the man's world)
f) Programmes which would help them to realize their capacities and potentialities.

g) Programmes which would enhance their vision and rights.

h) Programmes which would empower them and conscientise them.

The reinforcing principles of working with deprived and the neglected, particularly the dalits, tribals and the women are -

1) The researcher or the social worker (or, even the political worker) should go to them, lend them ears and not just voice. They should also start living with them - so as to get a real feel of the surrounding or the socio-political atmosphere they are in. Empathy is definitely a much powerful tool than sympathy.

2) With this aim in mind, the researcher or the social/political worker must also learn their day-to-day language and mode of expression; their songs and dances and other art forms; and imbibe their culture, thinking and presuppositions. We can, thus, become sensitive to their problems and needs, respect their specialities and potentials and accept their weaknesses and shortcomings.

3) Planning for the people has to be, necessarily, in full co-ordination with the people. After all, they *only* can know best what all are really good and necessary for them.

4) Ultimately, "A" only can develop "A". Nobody can develop another. Others around - sincere, sympathetic and co-operative - can help and guide only. "A" only can plan and work for "A". However much "B" tries, "A" cannot develop. "A" can develop only when "A" is fully conscious and conscientized, only when "A" takes active and involved part in his/her own development and is allowed to take part in the planning for his/her development.

This crucial/vital element is missing in the planning and working for women's development (or, the development of the other marginalised people). That is why, their development and *true* development of the nation, as such, remain a far cry.

In a court of law the accused was asked by the judge, "Who are you? The accused, who belonged to a remote village beyond the hills, replied, "I am Jatru". "How do I know that you are Jatru?" The judge questioned further. Jatru was a little puzzled because he did not know what to say. He took sometime and then affirmed what he said earlier, "I am not lying sir, I am Jatru of the village Buti. See...., I am standing before you." The judge, was not convinced. He repeated his question, "Well, can you prove what you are saying is true?" Jatru scratched his head, thought for a while and then asked for a mirror. The mirror was given, he looked seriously at it and then exclaimed, "Yes, its me, the mirror does not lie, look at it sir." The judge was certainly amused but he did not accept the mirror as the legal proof of Jatru's identity.

The root-cause of all the conflicts between the oppressor and the oppressed is this non-acceptance/denial of the identity by the class/group that wields power of every type. All subaltern struggles are the struggles for this "snatched-away" identity.

A Naga student from JNU had once said "in my State there is no language," meaning that 'Nagami' has no script of its own like Bengali or Tamil; it is written in English, a borrowed script. But according to Rukamini Bhaya Nair, a linguist, "script is language made visible. Unlike speech which is innate and part of our biological inheritance and are scripts are invented and are part of our cultural repertoires." Of the six thousand or so languages in the world, only about hundred or so have scripts. She correctly draws our attention to "so great is the violence done to oral traditions in the modern Indian State that an intelligent young person at the end of the 20th century can still hold the entirely erronous belief that he does not really have a "language." The Guiness Book informs us that about 865 or so of those estimated 6000 spoken tongues come from India. It is because of this imperialism of script over speech that Hindi, the language of the ruling class, has been declared the language of the majority (in India); in reality, we all know, different languages are written in 'devnagri' script and are called Hindi.

Identity is not a problem unless somebody else questions it. The "questioner" is usually somebody who does not know you, who is not from your place. He may be a person in power, with whom you interact in a formal manner. It is through interaction with the other party that the person who is being questioned about his/her identity can begin to affirm it. Identity does not become a problem in the history of a people until their identity is being questioned or threatened by others (as we see in our present study).

An ideology gives legitimation to a social group. It may not be entirely logical, but contains emotional elements which are capable of moving men and women and giving them a feeling of security. So happens probably because it contains a summary of the past, explains the present, and foresees the future.

The ideology of the indigenous peoples in India, which has held them together till today, has been based on their concept of regarding the earth as the Mother, their symbiotic relationship with the environment and the animal kingdom; it has been rooted in their egalitarian principle of social system, and their sense of balance in man-woman relationship and their respective social rights.

Every ideology, worth its name, contains a vision of the future. This view of the future, which gives shape to the hopes and aspirations of the common people, is vital for the indigenous peoples of India who are, today, threatened with extinction.

Ideology, as an expression of identity, always contains a criticism of how power is distributed, and advocates a redistribution of power. Ideology and identity are always a political reality though they are *not* only merely that. The search for the identity of the indigenous peoples, implies a demand for a redistribution of the political power. Therefore, the State where, power is concentrated, is often identified as an enemy from whom power has to be wrenched out through struggle— violent or peaceful. " The affirmation of identity is a political act. But unless it is accompanied by efforts at reflection and experimentation in searching for economic models of development that correspond to the genius of the people, the political efforts are not likely to yield the desired fruit". (Indigenous Identity—one of the publications of the Bhuria Committee which was set up to ascertain the justification of the struggle for "self-rule" in Jharkhand.)

The migrant tribal girls working as domestic workers do get involved in the continuous process of search for a renewed identity - an identity that emerges out of a blending of the traditional and indigenous with the modern and urban. (We have drawn our readers attention to this process earlier). They have migrated, we now very well know, in search of that identity since their original identity is in question as a result of the loss of their age-old source of livelihood viz. land, forest and domesticated animals. Loss of livelihood causes a drastic change in the pattern and standard of living and that, in turn, leads to a revolution in their food, dress, lifestyle and other aspects of culture. These girls, thus uprooted, cannot really free themselves of the deep-rooted sense of belonging to their own culture. They fall into the whirlpool of a pitiable crisis of identity.

Notwithstanding this, we cannot stop this undesirable migration - nor is it desirable to stop. When people are robbed of their right over their means of livelihood, they, at least, should have the right to look around for alternative avenues.

But, what really is identity? What are its features or ingredients? What ultimately matters in the days of capitalist social formations are the availability of economic opportunities and the fulfilment of economic obligations. Individual or "communal" (adjective from community) identities are now, unfortunately, shaped and coloured by these pre-conditions only. Industrialization and commercialization are the landmarks on the road to "modernity", where all identities — whether regional, religious, caste or ethnic — get eventually merged.

Yet, the struggle will be on. The struggle itself is their renewed identity. Organising or working for the migrants/ displaced is an attempt at helping them to acquire this "new look" identity.

Bibliography

1. Agarwal and Narain, "Women and Natural Resources"(Social Action, 35/4).
2. Alok Sharma (ed.), "Women and Work: Changing Scenario in India (1993).
3. Augustine, "Social Equality in Indian Society: The Elusive Goal".
4. Bihar Tribal Welfare Research Institute, Bulletins.
5. Bihar Tribal Welfare Research Institute, "Educating the Pre-literate".
6. Bihar Tribal Welfare Research Institute, "Impact of Industrialization on Bihar Tribes".
7. Boserup, E, "Women's Role in Economic Development" (1970).
8. Chanana, K., "Socialisation, Education and Women: Exploration in Gender Identity".
9. Coonty, Stephanie and Henderson, "Women's Work, Men's Property" (1986).
10. DN and GK. "The Sexual Division of Labour", EPW, Aug 26, 1989.

11. DN, "Significance of Women's Position in Tribal Society", EPW, June 25, 1988.

12. Dubey, S.C., "Modernization and Development: The Search for Alternative Paradigms".

13. Everett, J.M., "Women and Social Change in India".

14. Fernandes and Menon, "Tribal Women and Forest Economy".

15. Fernandes, W & Gulati, E, "Development, Displacement and Rehabilitation".

16. Forward-looking Strategies of the Nairobi Women's Conference.

17. Geeta Menon, "Tribal Women: Victims of the Development Process" (1987).

18. Gerda Lerner, "The Creation of Patriarchy" (1986).

19. Jane Collier and Michelle Rosaldo, "Politics and Gender in Simple Societies: (1989).

20. K.S. Singh, "The Scheduled Tribes".

21. K.S.Singh (ed.), "Tribal Movements in India".

22. Kelkar and Nathan, "Gender and Tribe".

23. Kolom, V.S. (ed.), "The Uprooted:Developments, Displacement and Resettlement".

24. Manoshi Mitra, "Women and Class Struggle: A Study of Tribal Movements and Women's Participation in Bihar, India" (1984).

25. Mrinal Miri (ed.), "Continuity and Change in Tribal Society".

26. Narmadeshwar Prasad, "Land & People of Tribal Bihar" (1961).

27. National Institute of Personnel Management, "Industries Face to Face with Tribal People: the Case of Chottanagpur in Bihar".

28. Nirmala Bannerjee, "Indian Woman in a Changing Scenario" (1991).

29. Padminini Swaminathan, "Development Experiences in India" in Social Scientist,March-April, (1994).

30. Renee Hirschon (ed.), "Women and Property - Women as Property" (1984).

31. Roat, H.C., "Tribal Settlement System and Development Strategy".

32. Roy-Burman, B.K., "Indigenous People".

33. Roy-Burman, B.K., "Tribes in Perspective".

34. S.N. Roy, "Migrant Women Workers".

35. Sachchidananda, "Culture Change in Tribal Bihar".

36. Sengupta, "Population & Resource Development in India" (in Zelinsky (ed.) "Geography and a Crowding World").

37. Sethi, Rajmohini, "Modernisation of Working Women in Developing Societies".

38. Sharma, B.K., "Habitat Economy and Society of Tribal Care".

39. Sharma, "Poverty, Unemployment".

40. Singh, Vyas and Mann (ed.), "Tribal Women and Development" (1988).

41. "Social Change", Journal of the Council for Social Development.

42. Surajit Sinha, "Tribes and Indian Civilization".

43. Suresh Sharma, "Tribes and Civilizations.

44. Uma Chakravarti, "The Purity of Women is the Purity of Caste Hierarchy" (1990).

45. Vandana Shiva, "Staying Alive: Women, Ecology and Development" (1990).

46. Vyas & Mehta, "Changing Land Relations".

47. Walter Fernandes (ed.) - "National Development and Tribal Deprivation".

Appendix 1

Questionnaire for Young Migrant Women Workers in Delhi From Chhotanagpur

1. Age — (i) 14-18. (ii) 18-25. (iii) 25 & above
2. Working for how many years? (i) 1 year or less, (ii) 1-3 years. (iii) 3 years & more
3. Employers economic status ? Occupation? Family size?
4. How does the employer treat?
5. Why do you change employers? What kind of employer do you expect?
6. What was your wages when you started working?
7. What is your wages now? ... after how many years?
8. What are the other benefits you get? (i) good clothes, (ii), cosmetics, (iii) jewellary, (iv) good food, (v) accompanying family to restaurants, movies, holidays, (vi) education / learning/ vocational training?
9. Do you (i) send income home (part or full)?
10. You save for (i) your marriage, (ii) sisters' marriage, (iii) land (which has been mortgaged or to buy),

(iv) other necessities, (v) brothers', education, (vi) parents' old age, health?

11. Will you like to go back ? (i) After how many years? (ii) After saving how much money? (iii) to get married, (iv) to take care of parents?

12. How did you came to Delhi? (i) through Church/ parish, (ii) with friends/peer group, (iii) with family/ relatives?

13. Economic status at home? (i) farmer, (i) craftsman, (iii) landless labour, (iv) factory worker, (v) unorganised sector worker.

14. Monthly income of the family at village?

15. Size of family? How many able-bodied and working?

16. General picture of the village/community? (i) occupation (in general), (ii) average income, (iii) health & education status, (iv) health & education facilities, (v) job/income opportunities.

17. Why migrated?

18. Why migrated alone?

19. Why chose Delhi—so far away and culturally so different?

20. What will you do for earning when you go back to village?

21. Whom will you marry? (i) own choice, (ii) parents' choice, (iii) from Delhi or urban, (iv) from village, (v) from outside community?

22. What will be the reaction of your parents / community if you marry (i) of your choice, but from community, (ii) of your choice and from other community, (iii) a non-tribal, (iv) from mainstream?

23. Are your family/community happy with your

(i) income, (ii) their better living due to your income, (iii) your happiness, (iv) your new life-style?

24. In what ways you feel different from them or discriminated against by them?

25. Will you prefer to continue as domestic worker or opt for any other job/work opportunity? What other kind of work is your preference?

INDEX

L

M

N

O

P

R

S